Black Potatoes

The Story of the Great Irish Famine, 1845–1850

Black Potatoes

The Story of the Great Irish Famine, 1845–1850

Susan Campbell Bartoletti

Houghton Mifflin Company Boston

For Brandy, with love

The text of this book is set in Bell.
Book design by Lisa Diercks
Maps by Jay Evans

Library of Congress Cataloging-in-Publication Data
    Bartoletti, Susan Campbell.
    Black potatoes : the story of the great Irish famine, 1845–1852 / Written by Susan Campbell Bartoletti.
        p. cm.
    RNF ISBN 0-618-00271-5   PAP ISBN 0-618-54883-1
    1. Ireland—History—Famine, 1845–1852—Juvenile literature. [1. Ireland—History—Famine, 1845–1852.] I. Title.
    DA950.7 .B37 2001
    941.5081—dc21   2001024156

Manufactured in China
LEO 10 9 8 7

Contents

Introduction 1

∿ Chapter 1
Black Potatoes, Black Potatoes 5

∿ Chapter 2
We've an Extra Potato 17

∿ Chapter 3
Lend Me a Little Reliefe 32

∿ Chapter 4
A Flock of Famishing Crows 50

∿ Chapter 5
Only Till the Praties Grow 68

∿ Chapter 6
The Fever, God Bless Us and Protect Everyone 89

◦◦ Chapter 7
   A Terrible Leveling of Houses 104

◦◦ Chapter 8
   The Going Away 117

◦◦ Chapter 9
   Where Would the War Begin? 136

◦◦ Chapter 10
   Come to Cork to See the Queen 152

Conclusion 167

Map of the Counties and Major Port Cities of Ireland 173

Timeline 174

Bibliography and Sources 176

Index 182

Acknowledgments

It takes a *clochán* to write a book. I am extremely grateful to the many people who helped me along the way in completing this work: *Buíochas a ghabáil leis na muintir na hÉireann as a gcineáltas agus a bhfáilte liom;* Professor Liz Rosenberg, for her quiet, calm persuasion and generous support; Professors Libby Tucker, Tom Dublin, and Leslie Heywood, for their careful readings; the librarians at Binghamton University and especially interlibrary-loan goddess Helen Insinger, for her amazing patience and doggedness; Críostóir Mac Cárthaigh, Department of Irish Folklore, University College Dublin, Ireland, for allowing me access to the main manuscript collection and responding generously to my many questions; librarians at the National Library of Ireland, the County Clare Library in Ireland, and the British Library, Newspaper Library, for their assistance; *tá mé faoin chomaoin ag* Kim Allen, my Irish language teacher, for her friendship and expertise; Dr. Brett Yarczower and Elizabeth Partridge, for their medical expertise; George Pugh, photographer extraordinaire; my editor and friend Kim Keller, who saw the need for this book; my daughter, Brandy, for her good humor and assistance in research; my son, Joey, for his ability to put things in perspective; and my husband, Joe, for his unflagging support and willingness to live with a horizontal space usurper.

Introduction

In Ireland long ago, there were good times,

not your time nor my time but somebody's time . . .

TRADITIONAL BEGINNING TO AN IRISH FOLKTALE

IN 1845 A DISASTER struck Ireland. A mysterious blight attacked the potato crops, destroying the only real food of Ireland's rural population. Over the next five years, the blight attacked again and again. These years are known today as the Great Irish Famine, a time when one million people died from starvation and disease. Two million more fled their homeland and emigrated to the United States, Canada, and Britain. Most Famine victims were Irish Catholics, who comprised 80 percent of Ireland's population. Most lived in great poverty. Most spoke only Irish. Most could not read and write.

Though many Famine survivors refused to speak of their suffering and loss, others passed on their memories to their children and grandchildren, who later told the stories to field-workers researching the Famine. The field-workers wrote them down. In many cases, these records are the closest that we can get

At dinnertime, this Irish family prepares to eat a meal of boiled potatoes. The average family needed to harvest at least four tons of potatoes each year. PICTORIAL TIMES, FEBRUARY 28, 1846; COURTESY OF THE BRITISH LIBRARY, NEWSPAPER LIBRARY

to the experiences of ordinary people during the Famine years. Collected within one hundred years of the Famine, they contain extraordinary accounts of life in Ireland.

This book tells the story of the Great Irish Famine, through the eyes and memories of the Irish people. You will read about how they lived, why their lives depended on the potato, how they dreaded the workhouse, and how they feared and defied the landlord and his agent who collected the rent and evicted them. You will read the stories of children and adults who discovered the black potatoes, who searched desperately for food, who suffered from starvation and disease, and who died. You will meet many ordinary people as well as political leaders, public servants, and charitable groups who worked hard to provide relief for the starving Irish but who could not prevent a huge loss of life.

One of the saddest things about the Famine years is that for each horrible story, there is always another more tragic and dreadful. Yet for every tragic story, you will also meet people who held on to hope, who committed heroic acts of self-sacrifice, and who fought to survive and to preserve their dignity.

ILLUSTRATED LONDON NEWS, *AUGUST 12, 1848*

ᕲᑐ Chapter 1.

Black Potatoes, Black Potatoes

Health and a long life to you
Land without rent to you
A child every year to you
And if you can't go to heaven
May you at least die in Ireland.
—A TRADITIONAL IRISH TOAST

THE WEATHER IN IRELAND has always been fickle, but the weather during the summer of 1845 was worse than the oldest people could remember. First the July days burned hot, much hotter than usual. After several days, the hot spell ended and the weather turned gloomy, cold, and damp. For three weeks in August, heavy rains fell every day.

Behind this cabin, potatoes are planted in ridges, called lazy-beds. ARTHUR YOUNG, A
TOUR IN IRELAND, *LONDON, 1780; RARE BOOK DIVISION, LIBRARY OF CONGRESS*

The changeable weather made some people uneasy. They had heard reports
about potato fields that had blackened overnight in some parts of Ireland. They
watched their crops for signs of decay, but the plants appeared to be thriving,
with their tiny purple flowers, large flat green leaves, and sturdy stalks. The
people couldn't see the potatoes, which grew on stems beneath the ground, but
they prayed that the tubers were swelling, large and round.

In 1845 most of Ireland's rural population depended on potatoes as their staple food. From August until May, six million men, women, and children ate potatoes for breakfast, lunch, and supper, an average of seven to fifteen pounds per person each day. They ate potatoes boiled, roasted, and mashed with buttermilk and onions. They ate potato cakes, potato bread, and potato soup. Even the pigs, cows, and chickens ate potatoes.

Not everyone was alarmed by the reports of the blackened fields. Some people reminded themselves that the potato crop had failed in the past, but the previous failures were never widespread. They were partial failures, usually localized to a few counties.

Newspapers optimistically predicted an abundant harvest from the more than two million acres of potatoes that were sown. It was hoped that the harvest would be as plentiful as the previous year, when there had been so many potatoes that farmers couldn't sell them all. They dumped some in the ditches as they returned from market and left others to rot in the fields for fertilizer.

A GREAT CALAMITY

The potatoes were harvested twice each fall. The early crop, called new potatoes, was lifted in late August and the general crop, called old potatoes, was lifted in October. In County Cork, when it grew time to harvest the early crop, fourteen-year-old Diarmuid O'Donovan Rossa helped his family dig out the reddish-colored tubers. As his father lifted the potatoes from the ground with his long-handled spade, Diarmuid and his family saw that the new potatoes had grown to a good size, despite the unstable weather. It was a great relief.

Diarmuid, his sister, and two brothers shook off the soil from the potatoes. They sorted the potatoes into large and small, then heaped them into wicker baskets. Some were taken into the house to be eaten right away, but the rest were stored in a deep pit dug in the ground. The potatoes were dumped inside, then the pit was covered with rushes and clay.

Because new potatoes were dug before they reached full maturity, they were thin-skinned and did not keep as well as the brown, tougher-skinned old potatoes harvested in October. New potatoes were eaten first, and the old potatoes were stored to eat over the winter and spring months and to use as seed potatoes in the spring. Once sown, each "eye" or indentation on the seed potatoes sprouted into new plants.

Throughout the fall, the weather continued to be fickle. Some mornings were warm and pleasant, but by the afternoon, the skies turned gray and heavy rains fell. On breezy days, the wind carried a strange odor. Farmers watched their potato crops closely, but the plants seemed sturdy and healthy.

One October day, as time for the general potato harvest neared, the midday sun darkened. By night a thick blue fog covered the countryside. "The old people all said they never saw such a coloured sky before," said Mr. Foley, a farmer from County Wicklow. "The people went to bed in fear and dread that some great calamity was about to befall them."

The next morning a powerful stench filled the air. It came from the potato beds. Farmers and laborers hurried from their cabins and ran to their fields. With dismay, they saw that their plants were covered with black spots. "The leaves and stalks hung down as if dead," said Mr. Foley.

Desperately, the people tried to save the potatoes. They lit fires to purify the air, and they cut off the blackened leaves and stalks. But the plants could not be saved. As the farmers and laborers dug the potatoes, their fear turned to terror. The potatoes were rotten, black and slimy. They had died in the ground.

The failure of the general harvest *was* a great calamity. People tried to reassure themselves that they still had the early harvest, at least the new potatoes were sound. If they rationed them carefully, they would have the larger ones to eat over the winter and the smaller ones to plant as seed in the spring.

Then more disaster struck. News spread throughout the Irish countryside that the new potatoes were rotting in the pits. Diarmuid's family rushed to check their stored potatoes. "Our pit was opened, and there, sure enough, were some of the biggest potatoes, half rotten," said Diarmuid.

A VISITATION OF PROVIDENCE

As the farmers and laborers looked over their black potatoes, they tried to make sense out of the disaster. What had caused the potatoes to rot?

Some people remembered how dark the sky had turned just before the blight struck. Many people blamed the darkened sky on the fairies, whom they believed lived in the Irish countryside. They said that the dark sky occurred because the different fairy tribes were battling over the potatoes. Each tribe wanted the potatoes for themselves.

"They'd often fight at the time of the harvest," said one woman. "My father told me that in the year of the Famine, there was great fighting heard up in the sky, and they [the fairies] were crying out, 'Black potatoes, black potatoes, we'll have them now.' And the potatoes that year were all black."

Some people took precautions to protect their harvest from the fairies. The most sinister fairy was the *Fear Liath* (far LEE-uh), or the Gray Man, a musty-smelling, fog-covered man who frequented the coastal areas, high ground, and boggy hollows. To safeguard their potatoes from the *Fear Liath*, people sprinkled holy water and placed religious medals around the storage area.

Those who didn't take precautions were sorry. "My father had warned me," said Johnny Aherne, a farmer from County Limerick. "But I didn't pay him any heed. I piled the potatoes in the house and didn't bother to put any protections around them. I had no time for that. The next morning, I looked at the potatoes, and every one of them was black and not fit for eating. The *Fear Liath* had touched them and he hadn't missed a single potato."

Others called the blight a "visitation of providence." They believed that God sent the blight as punishment for the way some people had wasted the extra potatoes the year before. "It was God's Will to have the Famine come," said

These travelers brace themselves against a sudden gust of wind. Many people believed that fairies created the powerful wind as they passed from place to place. Daniel McDonald (1821–53) captured this phenomenon in this oil painting called Sídhe Gaoithe, *or* The Fairy Blast. COURTESY OF THE DEPARTMENT OF IRISH FOLKLORE, UNIVERSITY COLLEGE DUBLIN, IRELAND

William Powell from County Cork, "for the people abused fine food when they had it plenty."

Another woman, clearly ashamed, agreed: "The potatoes were left in the ground by some people and not dug out. They threw them in the ground on the headlands or in the ditches and left them to rot."

Diarmuid O'Donovan Rossa didn't believe that God had sent the blight or the Famine. "I don't want to charge the Creator of the Irish people with any such work," he said. For Diarmuid, the blame lay with the English landlords, the powerful and wealthy men who owned most of Ireland.

The potatoes were gone, but Diarmuid's family still had a small wheat crop, which they grew to pay the rent. As soon as the wheat was reaped and stacked, the landlord sent his men, called "keepers," to guard it, to make sure that the O'Donovan Rossa family paid their rent.

"These keepers stayed in [our] house till the wheat was threshed and bagged and taken to the mill," said Diarmuid. "I well remember one of the keepers going with my mother to the mill, and from the mill to the agent, who was in town that day to collect the rent." It was the agent's job to manage the landlord's estate and collect the rent money.

Later, when Diarmuid's mother returned home, she had no money left. The agent had taken every shilling for the rent. "I don't know how my father felt; I don't know how my mother felt," said Diarmuid. "There were four children of us there. . . . The potato crop was gone; the wheat crop was gone. . . . That, no doubt, was a visitation of English landlordism—as great a curse to Ireland as if it was the archfiend himself."

Diarmuid's landlord wasn't the only one to act in such a heartless manner. After the potato crop failed, many landlords feared that their tenants would not pay their rent. To make sure they did, the landlords confiscated the livestock and grain crops as payment. For the Irish families who faced starvation, English landlordism seemed to be a curse upon them and their beloved Ireland.

The Greatest Curse

The bitterness between the English and the Irish began centuries before the potato arrived in Ireland. Ireland lies off the coast of England, only a day's sail across the Irish Sea. Between the years 1169 and 1530, England tried to conquer

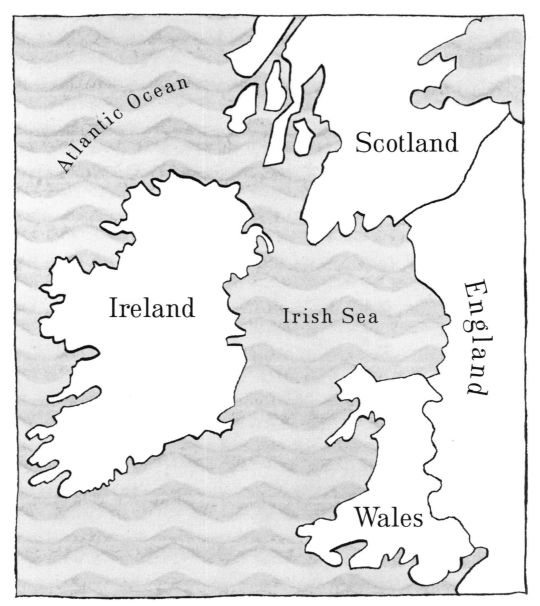

The island of Ireland is roughly the same size as the state of Maine—about 32,000 square miles.

Ireland many times, and many battles were fought between the invading English and the Irish. The Irish never managed to drive the English from Ireland for long. With each English invasion and conquest, the Irish hated the English all the more.

The bitterness that stemmed from ethnic differences between the English and Irish deepened as religious differences surfaced. In 1535 Henry VIII broke away from the Catholic Church and named himself head of the Church of England. In the sixteenth century, the idea of religious freedom did not exist. To maintain control over the Irish, Henry VIII and subsequent Protestant rulers tried to conquer and suppress Catholicism in Ireland. The conflict that had begun as English versus Irish now became English Protestant versus Irish Catholic.

Though Protestants and Catholics pray to the same God and share the same Christian church history, differences between the two faiths have resulted in much sorrow for Ireland. Over the next one hundred years, the British drove the Catholic Irish off their lands to make way for Protestant English and Scottish settlers. The British intended the settlers to bring a sense of order and civilization to the Irish, whom they considered rebellious and barbaric.

The Catholic Irish fought bitterly against the English colonization of their homeland, but in 1690, after Protestant King William of Orange defeated the Catholic Irish in a terrible battle at the Boyne River, it seemed unlikely that Catholic Ireland would ever rise to power again. To make sure, King William and the British parliament enacted a series of laws to punish the Irish Catholics and keep them powerless. The laws were called the Penal Laws.

Under the Penal Laws, Catholics were forbidden to vote, hold political office, carry or own firearms, engage in certain trades or professions, or provide their children with a Catholic education. They could not purchase land or bequeath their land as they wished. They were also forbidden to possess a horse worth more than five pounds.

Some Catholics converted to Protestantism in order to keep their land. Others

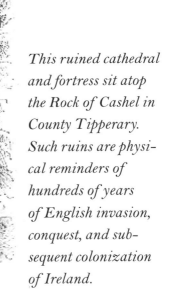

This ruined cathedral and fortress sit atop the Rock of Cashel in County Tipperary. Such ruins are physical reminders of hundreds of years of English invasion, conquest, and subsequent colonization of Ireland.

RICHARD LOVETT, IRISH PICTURES, LONDON: RELIGIOUS TRACT SOCIETY, 1888

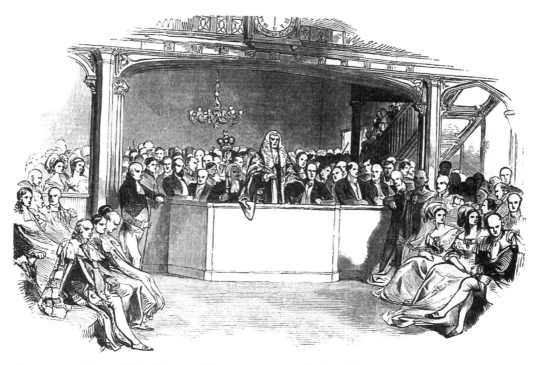

Representatives of the House of Commons stand before Her Majesty, Queen Victoria.
ILLUSTRATED LONDON NEWS, *FEBRUARY 8, 1845*

gave up their holdings and emigrated to America. Over the years, the Catholic lands were acquired by wealthy English and Anglo-Irish (half-English, half-Irish) Protestant families. The Penal Laws ensured that the Protestants remained the powerful landlord class and the ruling elite of Ireland.

Despite the laws, Catholicism thrived in Ireland. By 1800, 80 percent of Ireland's population practiced the Catholic faith. Though many of the Penal Laws had been repealed or relaxed, Irish Catholics did not have full political rights.

In 1800 the British prime minister William Pitt convinced the Irish elite to agree to the Act of Union. The act would formally unite England, Scotland,

Wales, and Ireland into the United Kingdom. Irish Catholic leaders agreed, believing that Irish Catholics would be granted full political rights.

When the Act of Union became law in 1801, the future seemed promising to Irish Catholic leaders. They looked forward to Catholic emancipation. They hoped that Ireland's economy would improve, now that Ireland was formally joined to Britain, the most prosperous and powerful country in the world. Irish leaders were excited about the prospect of sending representatives to the British Parliament, the legislative body that governed the United Kingdom.

They were wrong. Ireland was allowed to elect only a small number of representatives to Parliament, which gave them little legislative power. Irish Catholics had hoped to have their political rights restored, but this did not happen. Only members of the wealthy Protestant landlord class were eligible to take a seat in Parliament. This left Catholics, laborers, farmers, businessmen, and women without a vote.

The Catholic Emancipation Act was not passed until 1829, nearly thirty years after the Act of Union. Bitterly disappointed by the broken promises, the Irish resented the British more than ever. For the Irish, British rule and English landlordism remained the greatest curse.

ᏆᏇ Chapter 2.
We've an Extra Potato

Potatoes at morning

Potatoes at noon

And if I were to rise at midnight

Potatoes I'd get.

— Nineteenth-century children's chant

T O MANY PEOPLE, IRELAND seemed a land of plenty. The emerald green island had plenty of fertile farmland, green fields, raised bogs, lakes, and rivers. Trimmed by gracefully sloping mountains, Ireland had over two thousand miles of coastline.

Ireland had plenty of people. By 1845, the population numbered over eight million, making the small island the most densely populated country in Europe. "The population was three or four times thicker before the Famine," said Barney

During hard times, destitute families traveled the roads, begging for food and money.
PICTORIAL TIMES, *FEBRUARY 14, 1846; COURTESY OF THE BRITISH LIBRARY, NEWSPAPER LIBRARY*

Gargan from County Cavan. "There was a house on nearly every four acres of land around here, and some people had only two acres, and some had only one."

Ireland also had plenty of poor people: about three million farm laborers lived in great poverty. Travelers were appalled at the laborers' wretched housing, the poorly clad men and women, and the huge numbers of barefoot, nearly naked children. How could such conditions exist, considering that Ireland was administered by Britain, the most powerful and prosperous country in the world?

THEIR ONLY ENEMY

Ireland's poverty was blamed on the land system. In 1845 the Industrial Revolution had not yet reached Ireland, bringing new factory and mill jobs the way it had in Britain and the United States. Most Irish people made their living from the land.

The land system divided the people into three classes: wealthy and powerful landowners (called landlords), farmers, and farm laborers. The landlords owned huge estates, some as large as sixty thousand acres or more. Though a small number of landlords lived in sprawling country houses and even castles in Ireland, most preferred to live in England. These absentee landlords hired agents to manage their estates. Since many absentee landlords were only interested in collecting the rent, they never improved their property. Many estates fell into disrepair.

The landlords subdivided their estates and rented parcels of land to farmers. Farmers were classed according to the amount of land they held: "large" farmers rented thirty or more acres; "middling" farmers rented ten to thirty acres; and "small" farmers rented two to ten acres. In areas where landlords were absent, the large farmers held power and status.

A large farmer made a comfortable living, usually from dairy and livestock farming, whereas a middling farmer had a modest income. In addition to rent, all large farmers and those middling farmers who held a sizable amount of land were also required to pay taxes to support the local workhouse, which provided shelter and meals for the destitute. To help meet expenses, farmers subdivided their holdings into small plots and rented them to small farmers and farm laborers.

Small farmers struggled to make enough to survive. But the poorest class of

Some resident landlords lived in country houses. This house belonged to the family of author Maria Edgeworth in Edgeworthstown, County Longford. RICHARD LOVETT, IRISH PICTURES, *LONDON: RELIGIOUS TRACT SOCIETY, 1888*

Irish were the farm laborers. The farm laborers rented tiny plots of land, ranging from one-eighth of an acre to two acres. A laborer didn't need much land if potatoes were grown. No other crop yielded so much healthful food in so little space. Even the poorest families could thrive as long as they had shelter and enough potatoes.

In addition to potatoes, some laborers grew cash crops such as wheat, barley, or oats, which they sold to help pay the rent. Laborers were also expected to work for the farmer or landlord, even if it meant neglecting their own crops at planting or harvest time. Most worked about eighty days a year for the landlord or farmer.

Laborers lived in one- or two-room mud cabins, which they built themselves. Each cabin had a thatched roof, thick walls made of straw and clay, and a tempered clay floor. Often, two families shared a cabin, using a dresser or cupboard to divide the living space. Bundles of straw or a tick mattress stuffed with chaff or rags served as a bed.

Animals often shared the living space, too. Hens sometimes lived in the lower part of a dresser, while the family's pig grunted contentedly on a straw bed in the corner of the cabin. The pig was jokingly referred to as "the gentleman who paid the rent," since the money earned from the pig's sale at market was also put toward the rent. As one man jested, "We live on praties [potatoes] and point." By "point," he meant the family pig, at which most families could only point as they ate their potatoes.

Tenants paid high rent twice a year, on "gale-day," just after the first grain harvest in May and the last potato harvest in November. Small farmers and laborers considered it a miracle if they managed to cover the rent. "Their only enemy was the landlord or his agent," said Sean O'Dunleavy. "When gale-day came about, the rent was demanded and in some cases, there was distress and evictions."

Yet even tenants who paid their rent were not secure. Without rights and the security of a lease, they could be evicted at any time. Some evicted tenants found shelter with neighbors, but others joined the large ranks of the landless laborers who traveled from farm to farm, looking for work. Most landless laborers found work only during the planting and harvest seasons—at most, about five or six months each year.

In this small tenant farmer's cabin, the early potatoes are stored in the loft.
PICTORIAL TIMES, *FEBRUARY 7, 1846; COURTESY OF THE BRITISH LIBRARY, NEWSPAPER LIBRARY*

Landless laborers needed shelter and a scrap of land on which to plant potatoes. One common shelter was a *scalp,* which was built in a ditch. The landless laborer scooped out the earth, making room to stand, then roofed over the dirt sides and thatched the roof with rushes or branches. "Some men were very

These two women belong to the class of landless laborers. They live in a scalp, a shelter built in a ditch and roofed over with thatch. ILLUSTRATED LONDON NEWS, *DECEMBER 29, 1849*

clever at building such homes," said Ned Buckley. "No wind could penetrate those walls and they were warm and cosy, if not airy."

Bog squatters lived in huts built on the swampy bog. To a passerby, the sunken huts were barely distinguishable. When one doctor was summoned to treat a bog squatter, he climbed a slight elevation to look for the patient's hut. Suddenly, a voice shouted to him: "Arrah, doctor! Come down off the roof. The patient's inside!"

The startled doctor climbed down and found the hut opening. Inside, his patient lay on a bed of straw in a damp, smoky, but warm little room, heated by a small peat fire. The hut boasted a little table, three stools, a pot, and a shelf of chipped plates and mugs.

THE LANGUAGE OF HONOR

Before the Famine years, life was harsh for the Irish laborers, but not joyless. They traveled great distances to attend weddings, funerals, markets, county fairs, races, and hurling matches (a game resembling field hockey). On Sundays, they attended Mass in their parish church and throughout the year, they celebrated holy days such as Saint Patrick's Day, Easter, Christmas, and New Year's.

The first of February marked Saint Brigid's Day, the patron saint of dairy, and the start of the planting season. As the ground warmed, men and boys turned the mossy earth with their spades and sowed the seed potatoes. Women and girls maintained the potato beds, making sure the ridges remained firm and breaking up clods of earth. They churned butter, baked oaten cakes, carried water, knitted and sewed, and minded the youngest children. Older children tended the garden, scared birds away from the crops, and fed the pig, cow, and chickens.

After the potatoes were sown, the laborers went to the bog to cut turf to use as their winter fuel. Tiny white flowers covered the spongy wetland made up of decayed plants and trees. "Down eight or ten feet where the blue clay was, we'd get the good stuff," said James Hughes. "It was soft and slippery like soap. You could cut it out like a brick. . . . After it was dug, we would lay it out in rows to dry."

Once the turf had dried and hardened in the sun, it was carted home, heaped

At an Irish wake, family and guests combine mourning and merry-making. Here, the women "keen," or wail, over the body while the men sit nearby, drinking and telling stories. HARPER'S WEEKLY, MARCH 15, 1873; COURTESY OF THE LIBRARY OF CONGRESS

outside the cabin door, and covered with straw to keep it dry. With a turf fire in the hearth and an adequate supply of potatoes, even the poorest family was assured of warmth and full stomachs all winter.

The Irish people have always loved good times with family and friends. At night, they searched for neighborly hearths. They gathered in cabins, fiddling, dancing, singing, and telling stories about ghosts, fairies, and brave Irish heroes and their feats in battle. Most children knew Ireland's proud history before they even started school.

During times of plenty, women sold eggs, butter, and extra potatoes at small markets like this one. The few pence helped to buy oatmeal during the summer months, when the new potato crop wasn't ready to harvest. THACKERAY, THE IRISH SKETCHBOOK, *LONDON: SMITH, ELDER, AND CO., 1865*

In the rural areas, nearly two million laborers spoke Irish. Though some knew English, they spoke it only when the landlord or government authorities came around. "The Irish language was the language of honor," said Diarmuid O'Donovan Rossa. "It was the language of the table, the language of the milking barn, the language of the sowing and reaping, the language of the mowing, the *meithal* [cooperative labor group], and the harvest-home."

Children attended schools called "hedge schools." On warm days, the schoolmaster held classes outdoors, on the shady side of a hedge. On other days, classes were held in scalps or mud cabins or farmers' barns. Classes met early in the morning, six days a week, Monday through Saturday. Some landlords created schools on their estates for their tenants' children to attend.

Boys received more education than girls, and more children attended school in summer than winter, since they lacked warm clothing. Textbooks were scarce. In one hedge school, thirty students shared eight spelling books, four reading primers, and a handful of catechism books.

Parents paid quarterly fees to the schoolmaster. The fees depended on the subject, ranging from two shillings and two pence (about forty-six cents) for reading and spelling to four shillings and four pence (about ninety-three cents) for arithmetic. In some areas, parents paid the schoolmaster in turf, butter, and eggs, and provided him with lodging and meals.

The National School system was established in 1831. It provided free primary education, but at a price: the Irish language was forbidden, and English history replaced Irish history in the curriculum. Though many hedge schoolmasters became part of the National School system, they often refused to follow the curricula set by the Board of Education.

The Irish laborers married young—girls as young as sixteen, and boys slightly older. Newly married couples moved into small mud cabins, hastily built on a small patch of land and furnished only with a pot, a stool, and perhaps a straw bed. The Irish loved children, and large families naturally followed.

Storytellers had an incredible, practiced memory. In stories, ballads, and poems, they recited Ireland's proud history. ILLUSTRATED LONDON NEWS, *DECEMBER 21, 1850*

Although the British criticized the Irish for early marriages and large families, a sympathetic Catholic bishop explained it this way: "They cannot be worse off than they are and . . . they may help each other."

The Irish did help each other. As children grew into adults with families of their own, they often cared for their aged parents, who usually lived with the youngest child. As one woman put it, "It's easy to halve the potato where there's love."

The Irish were known as clannish and tough, but generous and kind. No matter how poor a family's circumstances, they never turned away a guest, whether a traveler or a beggar. They considered Christ to be in the person of every guest, and to close the door against a guest was to risk having Christ close the door on them. A line from an old song illustrates this custom: "We've an extra potato right hot on the fire, for one who travels through wet bog and mire." In return, beggars said prayers for the soul of their benefactors.

The Irish were devout in their Catholic faith, but they also believed that fairies—the "good" or "little" people—lived in abandoned houses, among the rocks and hills, and in the sea. They respected the fairies' sacred bushes and didn't disturb the fairies' mounds. They pacified the fairies' quick tempers by setting out food, leaving the last bit of crumbs or butter, sweeping the hearth clean, shouting a warning before throwing water outside (especially water used for washing feet), and keeping a bit of light burning at night. "If you mind these things," said Pete Hefferman, "you'll never be troubled with them."

THE HUNGRY MONTHS

The hardy potato had one downfall: it didn't last from season to season. At most, the harvest lasted about nine months. By May, when families had eaten the last of their stored potatoes, they faced the summer months, a time of hardship known as the "hungry months," since crops weren't ready yet.

During the hungry months, the men and older boys left home to look for farm work, often traveling as far as England. Women, girls, and younger children stayed home, tending their small gardens and picking berries, nettles, and wild cabbage to eat. The poorest families traveled the roads, begging from place to place. Out of pride, most families didn't beg near their homes.

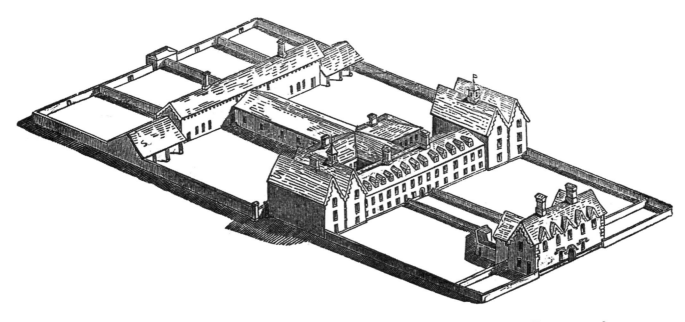

This sketch shows a typical workhouse complex in Ireland. The high walls prevented inmates from leaving without permission. S. C. HALL, IRELAND, 1841–43, VOL. 3, LONDON: HALL, VIRTUE, AND CO., 1860; COURTESY OF THE RARE BOOKS DIVISION, LIBRARY OF CONGRESS

As a last resort, the absolutely destitute turned to the local workhouse, also called the poorhouse. Under the Poor Law Act of 1838, Ireland's thirty-two counties were subdivided into 130 Poor Law unions. Each union built a workhouse to provide shelter and food for the destitute. The workhouse was administered by a locally elected Board of Guardians. Most board members were landlords or their agents.

The workhouses resembled a cross between a military barracks and a jail. The grim buildings were surrounded by high walls and locked gates. Each workhouse varied in size, accommodating from two hundred to two thousand inmates.

The Irish people feared the workhouse, with its harsh and degrading conditions. "The poorhouses were dreadful," said William Keane, a farmer from County Westmeath. "People hated to have to go in. . . . The paupers, as the poor were called, were badly treated. The food was poor and stingy. Those over them [the staff] had no feeling."

Upon admission, family members were separated and sent to different wards. Each person was bathed, issued a rough workhouse uniform, and assigned a place to sleep. They were fed two bland meals a day, usually milk, bread, oatmeal "stirabout," or porridge, and potatoes, when available.

The workhouse rules were as strict as prison rules. Children and adults had to rise, go to bed, and attend meals on time. Inmates were forbidden to talk during mealtime, swear, play cards, smoke, or drink alcohol.

All able-bodied workhouse inmates labored, usually at some tedious task. Men and boys ground corn, broke stones, or worked on the grounds. Women and girls scrubbed floors, knitted and sewed, washed linen, and tended the sick or elderly inmates and young children. Children attended classes and received some sort of training. Girls, for instance, were taught to perform the duties of a domestic servant.

Although people entered the workhouse voluntarily, they could not leave the grounds or quit the workhouse without permission. If inmates were caught escaping while wearing the workhouse uniform, they were charged with stealing.

To finance the workhouse, landlords and farmers paid Poor Law "rates," or taxes. During hard times, some landlords provided their tenants with food and opportunities to earn wages. Other landlords believed that the workhouses fulfilled any obligation they might have.

One landlord was known for telling those who asked for food to "get away to hell." After a workhouse was built in his union, he told them to "get away to the poorhouse." One woman noted the change, remarking wryly, "The poorhouse must have been a great saving on souls. Before, it was 'go to hell.' Now, it is 'go to the poorhouse.'"

ᘒ Chapter 3.
Lend Me a Little Reliefe

May there always be work for your hands to do

May your purse always hold a coin or two

May the sun always shine on your windowpane

May a rainbow be certain to follow each rain

May the hand of a friend always be near you

And may God will your heart with gladness to cheer you

— TRADITIONAL IRISH BLESSING

THE POTATO CROP FAILURE of 1845 hit the six million farm laborers hardest of all. Work was scarce in Ireland, especially after the harvest season ended. They depended on the potato harvest to carry them through the winter and spring. For them, the hungry months of summer stretched into fall.

Men, women, and children scoured the fields, roadsides, and ditches, foraging for weeds, nettles, and cabbage leaves. They dug for turnips missed by the harvesters. They picked over discarded turnip tops and bottoms, looking for edible pieces to take home. The pieces didn't boil into much, but they staved off the hunger pains for a little while.

Many people foraged at night. For some, it was to hide their shame at not having enough food for their family. For others, it was because they were stealing. When one farmer investigated a suspicious sound in his garden, he discovered his neighbor digging up turnips. Dismayed, the farmer asked, "Why do you come by night to take what I gladly would have given by day?" The neighbor replied, "I was too ashamed to let anyone know I was in such want."

As people grew hungrier, they became more daring. "The men used to steal the tails of the bullocks [the young bulls or castrated steers]," said one woman from County Westmeath. "They would wait until the landlord was gone to bed, then steal out and cut off the tails. They would skin them and roast them."

Men banded together and walked miles, looking for cattle. Once they found a herd, they cornered a cow. While a few men held the cow, another cut a vein in its neck, drained off a few pints of blood into a vessel or leather pouch, then pinned the incision closed. The cows weren't hurt from the bleeding: as much as one quart could be taken without serious injury. The men carried the blood home to their wives, who fried it with mushrooms and cabbages or cooked it in black pudding. The blood, rich in iron and protein, served as a meat substitute.

As winter approached, the cost of flour, oatmeal, and other foods skyrocketed. Merchants and shopkeepers bought up flour and oatmeal, then sold it in small quantities at double the cost.

To buy food, Irish laborers sold their furniture, bedding, and extra clothing. They sold their pigs, chickens, and cows, and even pawned their tools and fishing nets—anything at all to get money to buy food. When they had nothing left to sell, they borrowed money from moneylenders, called "gombeen men," who charged outrageous interest. The rates ranged from 20 to 50 percent.

This woman uses a láí *(pronounced "loy"), or long-handled spade, to dig for potatoes in a stubble field. In the background, a mother cries over her child.* ILLUSTRATED LONDON NEWS, *DECEMBER 22, 1849*

Parents grew terrified that they wouldn't have enough food for their children over the winter. Priests offered up Masses, asking God to save the Irish people from disaster. Few laborers knew how to read and write, but those who did sent pleading letters to their church officials, asking for help. Priests often wrote the letters for their parishioners.

Many parents felt ashamed that they could not feed their families. John Mansfield sold his wife's extra clothing and his coat. When that money ran out, he wrote a letter to his clergy, asking for a small loan. "Reverand [*sic*] Sir Pardon me for letting you know my great distress," wrote John Mansfield. "I did not earn one Shilling This 3 weeks I had not one Bite for my family since yesterday Morning to eat And I am applying to you As a good Charitable gentle man to lend me a little Reliefe. . . . I will pay you the first Money I will earn."

Others begged government officials. "I am ashamed to tell you my wife, seven children and myself only ate one meal of potatoes yesterday," wrote another man. "Another this day. We had two eggs in the house last night which my wife was obliged to get up and give the children to prevent them crying. And our last meal of potatoes is now in the house."

The letters and reports about the crop failure poured into the British government, but the British leaders remained cautious and skeptical. Many didn't believe the extent of the crop damage and called the reports exaggerated. The Irish, they said, had always had a tendency to exaggerate.

Some British people criticized the Irish, saying that the people had brought the situation on themselves. They said that the Irish didn't work hard enough to improve their lives. They blamed the Irish for marrying too young, having too many children, depending too much on potatoes, and listening to the poor advice of their priests. One Kerry landlord even called the potato destruction "a blessing to Ireland," while others claimed that the crop failure was an act of God, designed to reduce the Irish population to realistic levels.

These attitudes reveal the ethnic and religious prejudices that divided the

English and Irish people. Unfortunately, many British leaders and landlords allowed these attitudes to affect the way they dealt with the Irish people and the food crisis during the Famine years.

THE SCIENTIFIC COMMISSION

The British prime minister Sir Robert Peel was no stranger to the Irish or Irish hunger. In 1816 he served as secretary to Ireland, and he witnessed Irish hunger firsthand when a blight destroyed a portion of the potato crop. Peel established government soup kitchens and public works that gave the destitute the opportunity to earn wages by breaking stones, building roads, and digging ditches.

From his experience during the 1816 food crisis, Peel knew that life for the Irish laborers would get worse before it got better. He feared that desperate, starving people might resort to crime. He also knew that periods of famine were always followed by deadly, highly contagious diseases such as typhoid fever, cholera, and dysentery. There was no doubt about it: the Irish needed relief.

Sir Robert Peel had always been a cautious man, slow and careful to act. Before he sent relief to Ireland, he wanted facts. In late October 1845, he established a Scientific Commission and sent three scientists to Ireland to gather accurate information about the extent of the crop damage and to examine the potatoes. He hoped that they would discover a way to save the crop.

Today, we know that a fungus called *Phythophthora infestans* was to blame for the crop failure, a fungus so powerful that it destroyed entire potato fields within hours. We also know that the fungus came from an American continent, possibly in cargoes of guano fertilizer from South America. Some Irish farmers bought the fertilizer to spread on the potato fields.

Once the fungus reached Ireland, the wet climate helped the blight to spread. Wind and water transported its spores across the island, at a rate of fifty miles a day. When the spores fell, they germinated on the leaves and stems of the

Sir Robert Peel addresses representatives in the House of Commons, Westminster, London. ILLUSTRATED LONDON NEWS, *JANUARY 31, 1845*

The illustration on the left shows the remains of the seed potato, which has sprouted into a new potato plant. Underground runners have swelled into round tubers, or potatoes. The illustration on the right shows a diseased potato plant. ILLUSTRATED LONDON NEWS, AUGUST 29, 1846

potato plants. The rain washed the spores into the soil, and as the potatoes were dug, the spores spread.

Peel's scientists did not know about the fungus in 1845, and they misdiagnosed the cause as "wet rot." Insisting that the potatoes could be salvaged, the scientists wrote complicated instructions that explained how to care for the potatoes and circulated them throughout Ireland.

This family watches forlornly as a neighbor carries a basket of black potatoes. Despite the advice of scientists, the laborers could not salvage enough to feed their families.

PICTORIAL TIMES, *JANUARY 31, 1846; COURTESY OF THE BRITISH LIBRARY, NEWSPAPER LIBRARY*

Landlords, farmers, and parish priests explained the instructions to the laborers. Dutifully, the laborers did as they were told: they dried the potatoes in the sun, dug new storage pits, and used special packing materials made from mixtures of lime, sand, turf, and sawdust. They inserted rods to ventilate the pits. But the potatoes still rotted.

The scientists also claimed that the partially rotted potatoes were edible, if certain cooking instructions were followed. Again, the laborers dutifully listened: they separated the rotten potatoes into piles of bad and not-so-bad. Saving the latter, they cut out the black spots, grated the potatoes into a tub, and washed and strained the gratings twice. They squeezed the gratings through cloth, pressed out the moisture, then dried the pulp on a griddle over a fire. They mixed the pulp with the starch from the potato wash water and made bread.

No matter how the potatoes were washed or cooked, the people suffered from stomach cramps and bloody diarrhea. The potatoes were especially harmful to the elderly and infants, some of whom became so sick that they died.

THE CORN LAWS

Sir Robert Peel knew that the Irish laborers needed food—cheap food. From his previous experience with food crises, Peel knew that Indian corn is one of the cheapest foods that can keep people alive. Native to North America, the yellow cobs are also known as sweet corn or maize. Two pounds of Indian corn can make one stirabout supper for six people, once the hard yellow kernels are properly milled and cooked.

While the Scientific Commission studied the potato problem, Sir Robert Peel made a momentous decision: he decided secretly to import a huge quantity of Indian corn from the United States. He commissioned London bankers to purchase enough Indian corn to feed five hundred thousand people for three months.

Why the secrecy? When Peel imported the Indian corn, he was tampering with the economic philosophy of the British government. The philosophy is called *laissez-faire* (le-SAY fare), a French phrase that means "to let do" or "to let people do as they please." However, this term did not mean that Peel should have been allowed to do as he wished: general individual freedom is not what the British government intended when it practiced this philosophy.

By laissez-faire, the British believed that government should not interfere or exert economic controls in the free market of goods or trades. In other words, it was not the government's job to tell people how to run their businesses. The British attributed the strength and prosperity of their nation—as well as their own personal wealth—to their economic policy of "to let do."

The British government allowed one exception to the doctrine of laissez-faire: a set of laws known as the Corn Laws. In the United States, *corn* is understood as maize or sweet corn, but in Great Britain and other countries, *corn* refers to grain such as oats, wheat, barley, and rye. Because Britain wanted to protect the price of its homegrown grain, the government imposed high taxes on foreign grain crops—crops grown outside the United Kingdom. The taxes guaranteed profit for farmers and merchants.

Earlier in his political career, Sir Robert Peel favored the Corn Laws. Over time he changed his mind as he realized that the Corn Laws hurt the economy of the United Kingdom more than they helped. If the high taxes on imported grain were removed, then grain would be more affordable for people like the laborers, who formed the bulk of the population. The more grain they could afford to buy, the stronger the economy would grow. A strong economy meant that fewer poor people would rely on government charity such as workhouses.

When the Scientific Commission reported the extent of the crop failure, it estimated that half the potato crop was destroyed, though the damage was closer to one-third. Nonetheless, many laborers had lost their total crop. Peel knew that thousands of Irish people faced certain starvation unless something was done. The six million people who had lived on potatoes needed something

Seated on her throne, Queen Victoria formally opens a session of parliament by reading the "Queen's Speech." Her husband, Prince Albert, sits next to her.

ILLUSTRATED LONDON NEWS, *JANUARY 24, 1846*

else to eat. He wanted to feed them grain, but in order to do this, the Corn Laws had to be repealed.

Peel explained the dire circumstances to Queen Victoria and urged her to support the repeal of the Corn Laws. He told her that other countries—Belgium, Holland, Sweden, and Denmark—had suffered the same potato blight and that they had imported grain to sell at an affordable cost. He asked Queen Victoria to do the same for Ireland. It was the best way to stabilize food prices for the Irish people.

Twenty-six-year-old Queen Victoria was an agreeable and popular monarch. She reigned over the United Kingdom, but she did not make laws. Parliament made the laws. Although Victoria often spoke with government leaders such as Sir Robert Peel and helped to settle disputes, she felt it was her duty not to take sides. When Parliament members refused to repeal the Corn Laws, Victoria accepted their decision.

Parliament's decision angered Peel. "Good God," he said. "Are you to sit in cabinet and consider and calculate how much diarrhoea and bloody flux and dysentary [*sic*] a people must bear before it becomes necessary to provide them with food. . . ?"

Determined to provide relief for the Irish, Peel looked for a loophole, a way to get around the Corn Laws. He found one: since Britain had no existing trade in Indian corn, he decided that Indian corn was not affected by the Corn Laws. When Peel purchased the Indian corn, he took advantage of this loophole, even though he knew it would infuriate many members of Parliament, once they found out. It was a great political risk.

When the American cargo arrived, authorities stored it in two main depots at Cork and Limerick. The corn would be sold in the spring, when the food crisis would be the greatest. Even today, some people criticize Peel for this decision: they say he should have distributed the corn immediately, to relieve the suffering of the hungry Irish. They say he waited because he was more concerned about his own political agenda—the repeal of the Corn Laws.

In the meantime, Peel created a Relief Commission and appointed relief commissioners. The commissioners established local relief committees in each union and set up food depots. The commissioners sold the corn at cost to the local relief committees. Once the food depots opened, the committees would resell the corn to the people. The cost would be one pence, about two cents, for one pound of corn.

PEEL'S BRIMSTONE

Throughout the winter, the corn sat in the depots while Ireland's hungry scavenged for food and sold their belongings. As soon as the depots opened in March, people who had money rushed the doors and bought up all the corn. The penniless people were unable to purchase the corn. In Cork, the hungry crowd turned angry and threatening. Fearful of a riot, the relief commissioners called for the police to disperse the people.

The Irish laborers soon discovered that Indian corn is not a good substitute for potatoes. The hard maize kernels required special processing: the kernels needed to be chopped in steel mills, which Ireland did not have. To compensate, millers had to grind the kernels twice with regular millstones. Some British leaders complained about the special milling, since they felt that the Irish people should be grateful for any kind of relief.

Even after the Indian corn kernels were ground twice, the cornmeal was coarse and required presoaking and long boiling to make it digestible. "At first the meal was distributed in coarse lumps," said one man. "When it was boiled, it spat steam and boiling water all over the kitchen. The children had to be out of the room while it was being boiled."

Stirabout made from the coarse kernels harmed people who hadn't had a substantial meal for months. People suffered terrible stomach pains, and some bled

In this sketch, Cork artist James Mahony depicts angry people outside the food depot. When the depots opened in late March 1846, the Indian corn sold out quickly, leaving many people without food for their families. ILLUSTRATED LONDON NEWS, *APRIL 4, 1846*

to death when the hard kernels punctured their intestines. "It swells and takes the life out of us," said another man. Some people began to think that the British were trying to kill them.

The Indian cornmeal became known as "Peel's brimstone" because of its yellow color and its hellish effects on the digestive system. "Most folks said they'd rather starve than eat it," said one woman. "We didn't know how to cook it."

Laborers avoided the yellow meal as long as they could, but demand for it rose as hunger grew. The milling problem was resolved when already-ground cornmeal was imported instead of unground kernels. People also found that a mixture of cornmeal and oats was easier to digest.

Peel knew that the Irish laborers needed more than Indian corn: they needed the opportunity to earn money to buy food. He thought about all the improvements that Ireland could use—from new roads to new bridges to improved harbors and fisheries. He realized that the laborers could earn wages as they made possible these improvements. Peel began to make plans for a system of public works.

WORK AT ANY COST

It was nearly spring 1846 when Parliament approved Peel's proposal to provide public work for the Irish. Under the plan, the British treasury would fund some of the works, mostly in the form of half-grants to be repaid at a later date. Peel expected landlords to contribute most of the money for the public works, but they gave very little. Some preferred to organize their own works. They provided their tenants with opportunities to earn wages by building walls and digging ditches to drain fields and bogs.

Other public works were run by the Irish Board of Works, which looked after roads, bridges, harbors, and fisheries in Ireland. The officials from the understaffed Board of Works found it difficult to organize projects on such a large scale. They could not handle the thousands of applications that poured into their offices.

As whole families signed up, eager to earn money, the applications piled up unanswered. When the projects did not begin right away, angry laborers protested, demanding work so that they could buy food. Their demonstrations frightened officials, who worried that the laborers would turn violent. "Work at any cost," wrote an official, "was prayed for as the only means of saving the people from famine and property from pillage."

By the summer, the administration improved and over one hundred thousand people had work. Road construction provided the most common form of public work, since it was the easiest to organize. To reach the roadwork, laborers walked several miles a day, often on an empty stomach. Six days a week, ten to twelve hours each day, they leveled hills, broke stones, and hauled the stones away. They also built bridges and dug drainage ditches.

"The work was very hard," said Mick Kelly, whose father labored on one of the works. "But the work was a godsend to the people. The men had to be at their work from 6 A.M. to 6 P.M. in all weathers. . . . Sometimes all the ground that they'd clear in a day would be flooded with water the next morning, and the men worked in water up to their waists."

Many men worked all day without eating. "When dinnertime came, each worker washed his shovel, put some raw meal on it, and wet it from the water that fell into the drain and ate it," said John Hanrahan. "This was all they had for dinner."

An overseer, or "ganger," supervised the laborers. "He walked around, cracking his whip," said Brigid Keane. "If a man showed any slackness or weakness, he was knocked off [fired] at once. There might be one hundred men sitting on the boundary to see if any man would drop out." Workers were fined for faults such as arriving late or slacking off on the job. For each fault, the worker was "quartered," meaning he lost a quarter, or one-fourth, of his day's pay.

When men fell sick or died, their wives and children took their places. Like the men, the women dug drainage ditches and roads, broke stones and hauled

When men died or fell too weak to work, their wives and children took their places on the public works. ILLUSTRATED LONDON NEWS, *AUGUST 12, 1843*

them away. They carried away clay in baskets on their backs and wheeled barrows filled with dirt. Their young children crouched by the side of the road around small turf fires while they worked.

At first, relief workers were paid a daily wage, ranging from eight to ten pence a day, roughly the equivalent of sixteen to twenty cents. The wages were intentionally low to discourage laborers from applying for public works. Later the wages would be raised to one shilling, or about twenty-two cents. But even a shilling could not support a family as food prices soared. The wages also created a coin shortage: relief committees could not obtain enough coins to pay the workers. Long delays in payment resulted.

Some laborers worked for weeks without pay. When Denis McKennedy died, his wife testified that he had not been paid for two weeks. During that time, the McKennedys and their three children had only a few small potatoes, a head of cabbage, and some flour to eat. Another man, Thomas Malone, walked six miles each way to the public works in County Galway. He ate only one scanty meal a day. He died just before reaching his cabin one night, leaving bereft a wife and six children.

Throughout the spring, Peel lobbied hard for the repeal of the Corn Laws so that food prices would stabilize. By June, he won, but his success made him unpopular. When he addressed the house of Commons, members shouted and hooted at him. Realizing that he had lost the support of the Conservative party, Peel resigned as prime minister.

Peel never returned to office, though he continued to give support to the new government. Four years after his resignation, he suffered severe injuries after falling off a horse, and died. Though Peel has been criticized for acting too cautiously in relief efforts for the Irish, many people credit him with saving the Irish people from the worst effects of the potato crop failure of 1845.

Chapter 4.
A Flock of Famishing Crows

You landlords of Ireland I'd have you beware,

And of your poor tenants I'd wish you'd take care

For want of potatoes in the present year

From the crutch to the cradle they are trembling with fear.

—From "A New Song on the Rotten Potatoes," 1847

MANY PEOPLE SUFFERED DURING the first year of the Famine, but few people died. Peel's hated brimstone spared the Irish from the worst effects of the 1845 potato failure. By spring, as the days grew warmer and the ground grew ready for planting, people were grateful that the winter of 1846 was almost over.

No one believed the blight could survive the winter and affect the new crop, but still there was concern about the next harvest. Even if the potatoes were healthy, the harvest was bound to be small, since many laborers had eaten their seed potatoes over the winter. Those fortunate enough to have some left guarded them carefully. After one farmer's widow paid an outrageous four pounds (nearly twenty dollars) for two barrels of seed potatoes, she hid them inside a rick of hay. Each day, she removed one bucketful, enough for one day's planting. "She knew if it became known she had them, they'd be stolen for food," said Brigid Brennan.

Farmers and laborers planted the seed potatoes. Over the weeks that followed, they tended the beds. Potatoes need only a few weeks of steady sunshine, and sunshine was plentiful during the June days. The potato shoots pushed through the dirt and sprouted sturdily. The leaves unfurled, large and flat, and winsome purple flowers blossomed.

Though fewer acres were planted, newspapers once again predicted an abundant potato harvest. As the plants grew taller, farmers and laborers hungrily imagined the potatoes they would have come harvest time. They would eat them, toasted brown in the bottom of a heavy pot and mashed in milk or with egg and butter.

The poorest families would eat boiled potatoes, right out of the basket. With their thumbnails, they would peel away the jacket and dip the potato in a bowl of salt perched on a stool. A "dip-at-the-stool," the meal was called.

The British also rejoiced at the promise of an abundant harvest. At the end of June, Lord John Russell replaced Sir Robert Peel as prime minister. Deeply committed to the doctrine of laissez-faire, Russell believed that people should be self-sufficient and not depend on government charity. When the Indian corn ran out in early summer, he refused to import more, even though it meant that the laborers would have little to eat until the potatoes were harvested. After all, he argued, the summer months were the "hungry months," a time when Irish laborers were accustomed to less food and making do.

Lord John Russell addresses members of Parliament. ILLUSTRATED LONDON NEWS, FEBRUARY 15, 1851

Lord John Russell relied heavily on the opinions of another man, Sir Charles Trevelyan, who acted as permanent head of the British treasury. It was Trevelyan's job to watch over Britain's money. Described as a religious man of rigid integrity, Trevelyan worked hard to organize relief, but he did not want to interfere with the property rights of others. He believed that people should be self-reliant and not look to the government for handouts. He believed that God had sent the Famine to teach the Irish people a lesson, a lesson that would result in a new and improved Ireland.

At the promise of an abundant potato harvest, Trevelyan decided that the Irish laborers no longer needed to earn wages by means of the public works projects. He announced that the public works would close in mid-August, in time for farmers and laborers to harvest the early potatoes.

As it turned out, both Russell and Trevelyan acted too hastily. In early August, the summer heat wave ended and dark clouds filled the skies. It started to rain, softly at first, then heavily as thunderstorms rumbled. Fungus spores swirled in the gray, gusty air, traveling on the wind at a rate of fifty miles a day. The spores blew from east to west, then fell with the rain and washed into the soil.

To some people it seemed as though the fairy tribes were fighting over the potatoes again. "I was putting seed out in the ground and the ridges were all ready and the seaweed spread on them," said Old Deruane, a fisherman from Inishmaan. "It was a fine day, but I heard a storm coming in the air, and then I knew by signs that it was *they* were coming."

THE FAMINE WAS MAN-MADE

The potato blight struck during the first week of August of 1846, even more viciously than the year before. Three-quarters of the potato crop was ruined overnight. Many people lost their entire crop.

"My brother and I went up the hill to dig the potatoes," said Diarmuid O'Donovan Rossa, now fifteen years old. "He was the digger and I was the picker. He digged [*sic*] over two hundred yards of a piece of ridge, and all the potatoes I picked after him would not fill a skillet. They were no larger than marbles."

In shock and disbelief, this family regards their ruined potatoes. No one imagined the blight would strike two years in a row. PICTORIAL TIMES, *AUGUST 22, 1846; COURTESY OF THE BRITISH LIBRARY, NEWSPAPER LIBRARY*

A traveling priest reported devastation everywhere: "The wretched people were seated on the fences of their decaying gardens, wringing their hands and wailing bitterly the destruction that had left them foodless."

No one ever suspected that the blight could strike two years in a row. Over the previous winter, most laborers had sold or pawned everything they owned to buy food or seed potatoes. Now their potatoes were gone, and they had nothing left to sell. They had no Indian corn. They had no work.

Yet Ireland's fields teemed with grain crops—wheat, oats, barley, and rye— that could have been ground into flour and made into bread, stirabout, or oaten cakes. This remains one of the greatest ironies of the Famine years: while the Irish people were suffering from the loss of their staple food crop, a bountiful grain harvest was ripening. But the laborers could not eat the grain, for it belonged to the farmers and landlords. The hungry laborers watched as the grain was reaped, thrashed, and milled, then loaded onto wagons and driven to market, to be sold to England and other foreign countries.

Some historians claim that during the second year of the Famine, Ireland produced enough grain, livestock, wool, and flax to feed and clothe the Irish people. Other historians argue with this claim. They say that the exported foods could not have provided for so many hungry people. They point out figures that show four times more grain was imported than exported during the Famine years.

No matter how historians interpret the facts, this truth remains: while people were starving, ships filled with Irish grain and livestock headed to England and other markets. In the words of William Powell, this meant one thing: "Yes, the Famine was man-made. It was our rulers that saw to it that our food was shipped away to England from us, and left the people here starving."

It is difficult to understand how food could be exported from a country where people are hungry. One of the harsh realities about famine is that it is not about a lack of food; famine is about who has access to food. The British government did not intend for the Irish to starve, but they did not wish to enact laws which

The landlord's men drive the livestock to market, probably to sell to England and other foreign markets. ILLUSTRATED LONDON NEWS, *DECEMBER 29, 1849*

would interfere with the livelihoods of the landlords, farmers, shopkeepers, and merchants. If they did, they would violate the principles of laissez-faire. When the landlords and farmers sold the grain to England and other foreign markets, they did so because they believed that they had a right to make a profit.

Riots like this one in Dungarvan, County Waterford, took place as the Irish grew desperate for food or money to buy food. They occurred less often as people grew too weak from hunger and disease. PICTORIAL TIMES, *OCTOBER 10, 1846; COURTESY OF THE BRITISH LIBRARY, NEWSPAPER LIBRARY*

A military escort guards a wagon loaded with "meal," or grain, on its way to a relief station in Clonmel, County Tipperary. PICTORIAL TIMES, *OCTOBER 30, 1847; COURTESY OF THE BRITISH LIBRARY, NEWSPAPER LIBRARY*

To people desperate for food, the sight of grain leaving the fields was too much to bear, and serious riots took place. Five thousand people marched into Dungarvan, County Waterford. They threatened the merchants, ordering them not to export any more grain. They warned the shopkeepers to sell food at reasonable prices. When the militia arrived, the people pelted the soldiers with rocks. Soldiers fired twenty-six shots into the crowd, wounding several people and killing at least one.

In Pilltown, County Waterford, laborers armed themselves with sticks, rocks, spades, and hammers. After they attacked a mill, they marched down to Ferrypoint, probably to attack the barges filled with grain and livestock. They were stopped by a British naval boat filled with artillery and marines. "This arrival seemed to deter the country boys," claimed a newspaper, "and they again returned to their homes."

Throughout Ireland's countryside, men posted notices in public places. The notices announced meetings to discuss the food crisis. On a chapel door in County Tipperary, a notice warned laborers to attend the meeting or be "marked men." Trouble was averted when parish priests tore down the notice and told their parishioners to stay away.

As disturbances increased, the British government took strong measures. Along the Fergus River, the British navy escorted the ships and barges filled with grain and livestock. In Limerick, troops guarded the grain fields. Soldiers accompanied wagons on their way to market.

Guns and bayonets did not stop everyone. Armed with pitchforks and scythes, laborers ambushed and attacked the carts bringing the "English meal" away.

THE LABOUR RATE ACT

With 75 percent of the potato harvest destroyed, the British government was forced to admit that the food crisis was not over. Lord John Russell agreed to import additional Indian corn, but his late decision meant that the corn would not arrive until December. This left the laborers without an adequate food supply throughout the fall months.

Sir Charles Trevelyan also conceded that the Irish needed to earn money, but he did not want to spend British money on Irish relief. He decided that Ireland's ratepayers—the landlords and farmers—should take responsibility for their tenants and laborers. The Irish ratepayers should pay, not the British.

Parliament agreed, and they passed the Labour Rate Act in August 1846. Under the act, the cost of relief fell completely on the shoulders of the landlords and farmers. They were expected to pay additional rates, or taxes, to support the workhouses. The public works would begin again, but now the workers' wages would also be paid out of the rates. Food depots would be opened only as a last resort. Parliament agreed to loan money to each union, but they would not give any more half-grants. All the money would have to be repaid at a later date.

The British government intended for the Labour Rate Act to enable destitute laborers to earn money to buy food from shopkeepers and merchants. The government also hoped that the act would make ratepayers think twice before sending their tenants to the public works. The more workers they sent, the greater their union's debt grew, and the more rates they would pay.

It didn't work that way. The act had the opposite effect: many large farmers and landlords didn't worry about the debt because the rates were spread out over the entire union. If one ratepayer couldn't pay, he figured his neighbor would.

Once again, thousands of applications flooded the offices of the Board of Works. Once again, the understaffed officials were unprepared to deal with such large numbers. They didn't have enough pay clerks to administer wages or engineers to lay out roadworks and other projects.

As a result, work did not begin in many areas until late October or early November 1846. Even when the works started, more problems occurred because many overseers could not perform simple math to determine how much the workers should be paid.

In some places, there was not enough work for those who needed it. Nearly one thousand roadworkers, described as "emaciated spectres," shouldered their picks, shovels, and spades, and marched into Skibbereen. They protested that they could not earn enough money to buy food for themselves and their families.

Fearful of a riot, shopkeepers shuttered their windows and doors and sent for the militia. When the militia arrived, they did not arrest the protesters. Instead, the militia commander ordered the distribution of Indian meal and promised the laborers more work.

Mere Skeletons

Snow rarely falls in Ireland, but six inches fell early in November 1846. Icy northeastern gales blew across Russia and into Ireland, bringing hurricanes of snow. The snow fell throughout December, so deep it blocked mountain roads. Canals and smaller rivers froze over.

Winter was the cruelest time for the destitute and hungry laborers. They trapped mice, rabbits, badgers, and birds. They stalked through snow-covered fields, digging for edible roots. One man described a scene in a field: "Women and little children were scattered over the turnip fields like a flock of famishing crows, devouring the raw turnips, mothers half-naked, shivering in the snow and sleet . . . while their children screamed with hunger."

Over three hundred thousand workers trudged five to seven miles each day through snowdrifts, cut by icy winds. With spades in their hands, they showed up at the public works. In the bitter weather, men, women, and children huddled on the roadworks, many without shoes and coats.

Workers staggered from weakness and hunger, often not eating from morning to nightfall. They worked until they fell over their tools. "The strongest men were reduced to mere skeletons," said Felix Kernan, from County Monaghan. "They could be seen daily, with their clothes hanging on them like ghosts."

Hugh O'Hagan remembered how sorry his grandmother felt for the road-workers outside her house in County Down. "My granny said that she often took a pot of broth out the door," said Hugh. "The men would run for it and ram their hands into it, and it boiling, looking for the meat."

Meanwhile, food prices continued to soar. It soon took nearly five days' wages

In snow-covered fields, barefoot children dig for turnips and other edible roots to eat.

ILLUSTRATED LONDON NEWS, *FEBRUARY 20, 1847*

to buy one stone (about fourteen pounds) of cornmeal. For a family of six, the cornmeal lasted about three days. But food wasn't all the laborers worried about: they needed money to pay their rent or they faced eviction.

SKIBBEREEN

In County Cork, a popular magistrate named Nicholas Cummins heard reports that people were dying in large numbers in the remote hamlet Skibbereen. From November to December 1846, nearly one hundred men, women, and children had been found dead in the Skibbereen streets and cabins. Nearly two hundred more had died in the workhouse.

Some authorities called the reports exaggerated, but Cummins decided to investigate for himself. One week before Christmas, he loaded up a pony cart with bread and headed down the craggy, snow-covered road leading to Skibbereen.

When he reached the hamlet, he was struck by its desolation. The cabins appeared empty, as though everyone had packed up and left. No footprints were visible in the snow around the cabin doors. No smoke curled up from the chimneys. No hearth fires glowed orange through the cabin windows. No smell of turf fires lingered in the cold air. Not even a dog skulked about.

Cummins halted the pony and tramped through the snow to a cabin door. He pushed open the door and peered inside. At first, the cold, dark cabin seemed as desolate as the street. It had no furnishings—not a pot, a stool, or dresser—and the hearth was fireless.

As he turned to leave, he spotted several shapes huddled on a pile of filthy straw in a dark corner. "[They were] six famished and ghastly skeletons," he said. "Their sole covering [was] what seemed a ragged horsecloth, [leaving] their wretched legs hanging about, naked above the knees."

He thought the family was dead, but then he heard a low moan. "They were in fever," he said, "four children, a woman, and what had once been a man."

Suddenly, he heard a loud howling outside, and he saw that a "spectre-like"

In Thurles, County Tipperary, this plentiful market has grain and produce for sale,
but the starving people did not have money to buy the food. ILLUSTRATED LONDON NEWS,
AUGUST 26, 1848

crowd had gathered. Frightened, Cummins tried to push his way to his cart, but
the crowd blocked him. Someone grabbed his neckcloth from behind. As he
turned he was shocked to see an emaciated young mother, holding a newborn
baby in her arms.

Yet on market day, the Skibbereen shops were filled with meat, bread, and fish
for sale. It was a grim realization: the Irish people weren't starving because there
was no food. They were starving because they did not have money to buy food.

James Mahony sketched this bereaved family as they followed a funeral cart on its way to the cemetery. ILLUSTRATED LONDON NEWS, *FEBRUARY 13, 1847*

When Cummins returned home, he wrote a letter to the Duke of Wellington. In the letter, he begged the duke to bring the plight of the Irish people to the attention of Queen Victoria. He also sent a copy of the letter to the London *Times* newspaper. The letter appeared on December 24, 1846. It prompted wealthy British businessmen and merchants to form the British Relief Association, a charitable organization whose purpose was to raise money for Irish relief.

In February 1847 another newspaper, the *Illustrated London News*, commis-

James Mahony sketched this mother as she begged for money to buy a coffin for her dead baby. ILLUSTRATED LONDON NEWS, *FEBRUARY 13, 1847*

sioned a Cork artist, James Mahony, to provide an illustrated report on the conditions in Skibbereen. Mahony spent several days traveling throughout Skibbereen, and, like Nicholas Cummins, he was moved by the sights. "We either met a coffin or a funeral at every hundred yards," said the artist. "I saw the dying, the living, and the dead lying upon the same floor, without anything between them and the cold earth, save a few miserable rags."

Mahony sketched images impossible to forget: children digging for potatoes in a stubble field, a sick father lying inside a bare cabin, a grieving family following a funeral cart, a mother begging for money to buy a coffin for her dead baby.

When the *Illustrated London News* published Mahony's article and pen-and-ink sketches, readers were shocked and appalled at the extent of Ireland's famine and poverty. Reports about starvation and misery in Ireland appeared in other newspapers and magazines as far away as the United States. Readers responded generously and sent donations of money and clothing.

Though many British newspapers remained critical of the Irish, blaming them for their own poverty and suffering, the *Illustrated London News* tended to be sympathetic. One of its editorials shamed the British government, calling its relief efforts a mockery. "We have not done our duty by Ireland. . . . Neglect, carelessness, and laissez-faire do not make a cheap system of government, but a very costly one." The writer concluded with a stinging comment: "There is only one book the English believe in—the ledger."

Snow, sleet, cold rain, and misery blanketed Ireland throughout the harsh winter, yet many Irish laborers clung to the hope that the potato would return, healthy as ever. One faithful laborer carried a handful of seed potatoes in his pocket for safekeeping until he could plant them. In the meantime, he struggled to support his four children on the few pence he earned each day.

ᏪᏬ Chapter 5.
Only Till the Praties Grow

They sold their souls for penny rolls,
For soup and hairy bacon.

—Louis O'Malley, Edgeworthstown, County Longford

Some of the saddest stories of the Famine years are about parents who could not feed their children, or mothers who died with their infants still trying to nurse. As the food crisis deepened, people saw sights that they would never forget as long as they lived.

One shopkeeper remembered a mother who cradled a malnourished baby in her arms. "The poor little thing was gaunt and kept whining for something to eat," he said. He gave the mother some milk, but later that day, he found her lying dead by the roadside. The baby was still alive in her arms.

It was shocking to hear stories about families so desperate for money to buy food that mothers had to decide between feeding their infants and feeding their older sons, so that the latter might have the strength to work. "A man employed

In Ennis, County Clare, the Widow Connor prays over her dying child. The mortality rate was greatest for children under five and adults over sixty. ILLUSTRATED LONDON NEWS, *JANUARY 5, 1850*

on the public works became sick," the Reverend B. O'Connor told members of the Killarney relief committee. "His son, who was fifteen years of age, was put in his place upon the works. The infant at the mother's breast had to be removed, in order that this boy might receive sustenance from his mother, to enable him to remain at work."

It was even more disturbing to hear reports of parents who committed unthinkable acts of infanticide, murder, and suicide, rather than see their children suffer.

Such tragedies are difficult and unsettling to think about today. In 1847 a Quaker wrote sympathetically about how starvation affects the body and the mind: "Poor things! I can wonder at nothing I hear, after what I have seen of their fearful wretchedness and destitution. None of us can imagine what change would be wrought in us if we had the same shocking experience."

Until the potatoes grew again, the Irish needed to find food or money to buy food. For some, this meant turning to crime; for others, it meant turning their back on the Catholic faith. It wasn't easy for honest people to turn to crime or for devout people to give up their faith.

'TWAS NO SIN

Like all countries, Ireland had its share of crime—the usual debtors, beggars, prostitutes, pickpockets, and drunkards. Overall, Ireland had always been a tranquil country, with little unrest, and the Irish were law-abiding people. But now as the blight devastated the potato crops, hunger drove people to desperate measures.

Though some people participated in food riots and attacks on shops, most crimes were small, committed by people struggling to survive and provide for their families. Small crimes consisted of stealing food: potatoes, turnips, cabbages, meal, butter, or livestock.

Was it a sin to steal when you and your family were suffering from hunger?

Armed men wait to attack carts carrying grain and livestock. PICTORIAL TIMES, *OCTOBER 30, 1847; COURTESY OF THE BRITISH LIBRARY, NEWSPAPER LIBRARY*

Some priests told their starving parishioners that they should always ask for food first, but if they were refused and if they were in extreme need, then they should not hesitate to take food. Patrick Dempsey agreed, saying, "And sure, 'twas no sin, and you starving, to steal whatever you could to eat."

Some laborers stole food from farmers' kitchens. Thieves carried spoons in their pockets, and when they found an untended pot of gruel, they stole right from the pot. One County Wicklow man went into a farmer's house and helped himself to a leg of mutton boiling in an untended pot on the fire. "His family were hungry," said his granddaughter, Mrs. Kavenagh. "So, despite being scalded, he took the meat out of the pot and brought it home."

Children helped to keep their families alive. After wheat, rye, and oats were reaped and stacked, they sneaked into the fields to fill bags with grain. "You would never see anyone in the daylight," said Mrs. Gilmore from County Westmeath. "The grownups would stay in the houses and their children would steal under cocks of hay or stooks of oats and rye. . . . When night would come and they had their little bags full, they would steal back to their houses and boil the grains for supper."

After farmers planted their seed potatoes, people plundered the potato beds, using long sticks with a nail driven into one end. They jabbed the stick into the earth, and each time the nail struck a seed potato, they pulled it up. In other cases, as soon as the stalks appeared above the ground, people rooted out the potatoes before they were half grown.

Farmers protected their crops as best they could. They sat up at night to guard their turnips, cabbages, and livestock. They stayed home from church on Sundays. Some dug dangerous mantraps, or trenches, in their fields. The trenches, about eight feet deep and two feet wide, were concealed with brambles and grass. "People lay in wait and when the robber fell into the trap, he was pounced upon and beaten to death with sticks," said Thomas O'Flynn. "In some cases the trap held water and the robber was drowned."

Landlords hired armed watchmen to guard their property against trespassers. In County Mayo, a watchman arrested sixteen-year-old Tom Flynn for fishing in the river that ran through the estate. Tom later returned to the river and dumped lime into the water, poisoning the fish. "The fish floated, bellies up, to greet the gentry," said Tom's granddaughter, Elizabeth Gurley Flynn. Before Tom could be arrested again, he ran away and boarded a ship bound for Canada.

People convicted of crimes received harsh sentences, even for small crimes like trespassing. One woman received a three-day jail sentence for trespassing through a farmer's cabbage patch. An Ennis man was given a two-year jail sentence for sheep stealing, an activity he engaged in to provide for his wife and four children. While he was in jail, his wife and six-year-old daughter died from starvation. In County Wicklow, two boys caught stealing turnips managed to stash the bag beneath a bush. After serving a three-month jail sentence, the boys returned to the field, found their bag of stolen turnips intact, and carried them home in triumph.

Some convicted criminals were sentenced to "transportation," or exile. They were shackled and shipped to Australia, where they served several years of hard labor in the barbarous British penal colonies. One sixteen-year-old boy found guilty of stealing a cow was sentenced to transportation. The judge felt bad about the sentence, considering the boy's age, but he decided that young people must be punished when they broke the law. "Young lads like the prisoner should not be allowed to steal with impunity [without punishment]," he said. "The best thing would be to send him out of the country." Once transported, people rarely returned.

As the food crisis worsened over the winter of 1846–47, newspapers continued to publish reports about food riots, plundered shops, overcrowded workhouses, and whole families that perished in their cabins. Members of the middle and upper classes grew alarmed as they realized that jail and transportation weren't enough to deter criminals.

The news disturbed Sir Charles Trevelyan, too. At last, he faced the hard facts: the Irish laborers needed food. He decided to feed them soup.

THE SOUP KITCHEN ACT

Soup seemed an ideal food for three reasons: it was nutritious, inexpensive, and easy to make in large quantities. Served with a piece of bread or meal-cake, soup would provide a cheap but nourishing meal for thousands of destitute people.

People faced harsh punishments when they broke the law. This woman was arrested for trespassing in a farmer's cabbage patch. She and her baby were sent to jail for three days. THACKERAY, THE IRISH SKETCHBOOK, *LONDON: SMITH, ELDER, AND CO., 1865*

In February 1847 Parliament passed the Temporary Relief Act, better known as the Soup Kitchen Act. Once again, the relief was slow in coming. It took four months and ten thousand ledger books, eighty thousand sheets of paper, and three million soup tickets to establish the government soup kitchens.

At last the soup kitchens opened in June. For the first time, government food relief was available to the poorest laborers without having to enter the hated workhouse. They could remain at home and get food from a local soup kitchen. This was a significant difference, since it allowed the laborers to tend their potato beds, which would ensure food for the next harvest.

The soup was made in huge vats or pots, called boilers, and distributed at a temporary feeding facility, called a soup kitchen. "It was made from small quantities of meat but chiefly vegetables, nettles, and herbs," said Felix Kernan. "A quantity of the steaming liquid was given to each person daily."

People with ration tickets lined up outside the soup kitchens. Each time a bell rang, one hundred people were admitted and given a bowl of soup and a piece of bread. They hurried to their seats at a long table, where a spoon was attached to a chain, ate quickly, then left by the exit door. The bowls were rinsed, the bell was rung, and the next group was admitted.

Despite the strict rules, some starving people fought to get ahead of others and even snatched food from others. "When the crowds queued up, there was a man who was supposed to keep order," said Sean Cunningham. "He was most cruel and often beat unmercifully those waiting with a heavy cudgel or stick."

Once inside, ravenous people risked injury when they couldn't wait their turn. "The hungry creatures, often unable to wait until they were served, plunged their hands into the boiling cauldrons," said Felix Kernan.

In some unions, people walked several miles to reach the soup kitchen. Weak from hunger, some died along the road or fainted when they reached the entrance. Others died as they waited in line. Some people dropped dead as soon

In April 1847, a model soup kitchen opened in Dublin. Many well-to-do people inspected the kitchen and sampled the soups prepared by the renowned chef, Alex Soyer. ILLUSTRATED LONDON NEWS, *APRIL 17, 1847*

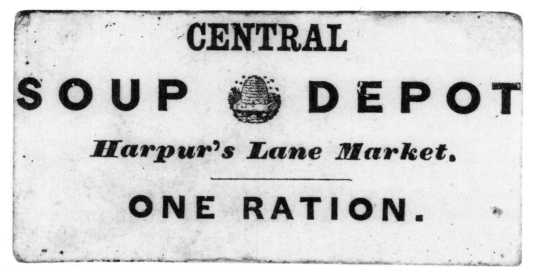

The relief commission issued ration cards to people who qualified for soup. Half-ration cards were given to children under nine. COURTESY OF THE NATIONAL LIBRARY OF IRELAND, R. 27159

as they ate, since the sudden intake of food often causes a malnourished body to experience shock.

Doctors questioned the nutritional value of a soup diet, claiming that soup alone did not supply the nutrients necessary for the body to maintain strong bones, muscles, and blood. A lack of vitamins contributed to outbreaks of diarrhea and a disease called scurvy, which caused teeth to fall out and bones to weaken.

A soup diet was especially harmful to people suffering from dysentery. Commissariat officers agreed with the doctors, complaining that the soup "ran through the paupers." Nonetheless, soup kichens replaced the public works as the main source of government relief.

'TIS BETTER DIE, MOTHER

Charitable groups and individuals also established soup kitchens. Although most benefactors gave generously and freely, a small number were evangelical Protestant zealots. They gave soup, money, and clothing only to Catholics who gave up their faith and converted to Protestantism. These evangelical Protestants were called "soupers," and their recruiting activity was called "souperism."

Overenthusiastic soupers went from cabin to cabin, urging the hungry Catholics to attend Protestant church services or Bible study classes in return for food. They printed religious tracts that criticized the Catholic faith and gave the tracts to children to take home to their families. The soupers also left the tracts in public places and tossed them along the road and into cabins, in hope that Catholics would read them.

Some soupers tried to force Catholics to break with their faith by serving soup with meat on Fridays, a fast day when Catholics were forbidden to eat meat. "Any Catholic who turned Protestant or ate bacon or beef on Fridays got as much soup and meat as they wanted to take," said James Argue from County Cavan. "But anyone who refused to eat beef or bacon on Fridays got nothing at all." Some people claim that soupers tied the hands of Catholic children behind their backs, to prevent them from making the sign of the cross before they ate.

When a Catholic farmer's wife heard about the souperism in her district, she decided to help her neighbors herself. "She started a rival kitchen on her own, to combat the hunger and the proselytism," said Mary Murphy from County Cork. "She gave of her beets, potatoes, sour milk, and oatmeal to her less fortunate neighbors."

Many people refused to convert, no matter how hungry or destitute. When one souper offered food to a starving woman and her son if they renounced their faith, the mother turned to her son and asked if it were better to take the soup or die. In Irish, the boy replied, "Is fearr an bás, a mháthair" ('Tis better die,

This rare sketch shows a Protestant "soup school" for starving Catholic children in County Galway. COURTESY OF THE NATIONAL LIBRARY OF IRELAND, R. 24718

Mother). Many devout Catholics agreed. "The Catholics in these parts died on the roads sooner than partake of the soup," said one woman from County Down.

But hunger drove others to give up their faith, at least for a little while. When one priest discovered that a former parishioner had converted, he admonished the parishioner, telling him, "You cannot please God and the devil." The parishioner assured the priest, saying, "Ah, Father, it's only till the praties [potatoes] grow."

In County Tipperary, converts were given new clothes in return for attending the Protestant service. The next Sunday, they wore their new clothes to Mass at the Catholic church. The Protestant minister demanded that they return the clothes, but the "converts" refused, claiming that they had fulfilled their promise.

According to Thomas Kelly, one poor Catholic family was on the brink of starvation when the mother "took the soup" for herself and her two sons. She attended the required Protestant church, but she followed the rituals of the Catholic Mass throughout the service. "She knelt on the floor and recited her rosary continuously while the minister officiated," said Thomas. The minister had a change of heart, and at the end of the service, he told her that she did not have to come back to his church.

Overall, soupers and souperism were rare, but where they did exist, they left a lasting and bitter legacy. They created great tension between the Catholics and Protestants and between those who took the soup and those who refused. Some people believed that those who took the soup left a curse upon their village.

However, it would be a mistake to think that people treated members of their own religion more kindly or more generously. Religious differences may have divided some people, but the opportunity to profit tended to unite them. Most Catholic and Protestant merchants, shopkeepers, and moneylenders were found to charge equally exhorbitant prices and interest rates.

Charity Must Begin at Home

Some resident landlords and large farmers had always helped their tenants during hard times. When the potato crop failed, they continued to use their own money and resources. They made soup and stirabout in their kitchens and doled it out on their estates. "The Marquis of Downshire was anxious to do all he could to relieve the poor on his estates," said Francis Mac Polin. "It was a common sight to see the poor running along the Briansford Road to Hilltown with their wee tin cans for their rations."

Much famine relief was performed by women, often the wives and daughters

of large farmers, landlords, and officials. Elizabeth Smith, wife o
Wicklow landlord, wrote in her diary: "Charity must begin at home. .
giving milk and soup to all our workmen and soup to all our sick and a
We must buy another cow for we are running short of milk and butter."

Some children helped others their own age. In Kilrush Union, seven-year
"Little Miss Kennedy," the daughter of a Poor Law inspector, saw children w
had only rags to wear during the winter months. She gave away her own clothes
then part of her mother's wardrobe. When that wasn't enough, she purchased
cloth with her own money and sewed clothes for the children.

Women established schools for local children. In "industrial" schools, children
studied reading and writing and worked at fancy knitting and embroidery. The
items they made were sold in London for the children's benefit. One observer
noted that a twelve-year-old girl often knitted all night to make items to sell.
The girl's work kept her family from the poorhouse.

Ordinary people with little extra for themselves helped others as best they
could. "Old Mrs. Cremin was very good and full of charity to the poor and hungry," said Ned Buckley. "She always boiled a lot of potatoes and put the leftover
ones near the fire for any hungry poor person who might chance to call the
house. A few potatoes half-cold and a basin of milk was a great boon to such
starving people."

"My mother's people lived in Gleann," said another woman. "The house was
near the road, and a pot of stirabout was kept for any starving person who passed
the way. . . . One day a big *fathach* [giant] of a fellow staggered in. He wolfed his
share of stirabout and made for the door, but there was a tub of chopped cabbage
and porridge for the pigs. He fell on his knees by the tub and devoured the stuff."

When parents died, brothers and sisters looked after each other, often com-
mitting extraordinary acts of self-sacrifice and heroism. When two orphaned
brothers, ages nine and five, knocked on a woman's door and asked for bread,
the woman gave the older boy a piece left over from her breakfast. "You must

"Little Miss Kennedy" distributes winter clothes to needy children in Kilrush union, County Clare. The artist hoped this sketch would immortalize the nine-year-old girl and inspire other people to give generously. ILLUSTRATED LONDON NEWS, DECEMBER 22, 1849

divide this with your little brother," she told him. Before she closed the door, she saw him hand the bread to his younger brother, saying, "Here, Johnny, you are littler than I and cannot bear the hunger so well. You shall have it all."

The Society of Friends, also known as the Quakers, was the largest organization to provide soup and food for the hungry. Members used their close ties with American and English Quakers to import rice and provide equipment to set up soup kitchens in many areas throughout Ireland. They contributed clothing and bedding, distributed seed, and encouraged the growth of new crops, such as flax, which could be sold. They also helped to develop the fisheries.

The British Relief Association raised donations for Ireland primarily through a letter-writing campaign. Queen Victoria contributed two thousand pounds (about ten thousand dollars), and other donations came from England, America, and Australia. Members of the British Relief Association worked closely with local relief committees and provided money, food, fuel, and clothing. They granted each distressed Irish union a sum of money that was used to provide two hundred thousand schoolchildren with a daily ration of rye bread and warm broth.

Many Americans felt sympathy for the starving Irish, and they held concerts, tea parties, and "donation parties" for the benefit of Ireland. Young women in boarding schools sewed clothing and other useful articles to sell. They donated the proceeds to Ireland.

Many southern railroads in the United States waived tolls on roads and canals for provisions headed to Ireland. Though United States government aid was not officially sanctioned, Congress gave permission for two naval ships, the *Jamestown* and the *Macedonian*, to transport food and supplies to Ireland. It was an exceptional gesture, considering that the United States was engaged in a war with Mexico at the time.

A remarkable contribution came from an American Indian tribe, the Choctaw Nation, which felt a special kinship with the suffering Irish. Fifteen years earlier, during the winter of 1831–32, the Choctaws were removed from their ancestral lands in Mississippi. During the "Trail of Tears," half their nation died on the six-hundred-mile forced march to Oklahoma. In 1847 they donated $110 to Irish relief.

The Society of Friends established soup kitchens throughout the most distressed areas in Ireland. They served 1,500 gallons of soup daily at this kitchen in Cork.

ILLUSTRATED LONDON NEWS, *JANUARY 16, 1847*

This grand military bazaar was held in London for the benefit of Irish relief. Noblewomen set up elaborate stalls and offered an array of fine good for sale. ILLUSTRATED LONDON NEWS, *MAY 29, 1847*

The greatest amount of money came from Irish emigrants already in the United States and Canada. They sent ten times as much money as any other group, often in the form of passage tickets to help their family members emigrate. In 1847 alone, they sent nearly a million dollars to their homeland.

An artist depicts the relief that the Irish people felt when provisions arrived. In some coastal villages, Irish fishermen rowed out to greet the ships. The ship's crew pitied the men and gave them food. PICTORIAL TIMES, *JANUARY 30, 1847; COURTESY OF THE BRITISH LIBRARY, NEWSPAPER LIBRARY*

THE FAMINE IS OVER

At first, many poor people hated the idea of taking free government soup, believing that it was degrading to accept charity. Some said they would rather starve, while others waited until nightfall to seek their ration. "The poor people, bad though their plight was, still preserved some of their dignity and often

The Jamestown *and the* Macedonian *(shown here) carried provisions from the United States to Ireland.* ILLUSTRATED LONDON NEWS, *AUGUST 7, 1847*

waited for cover of night before going for their meal of soup," explained Kathleen Donovan.

By mid-August 1847, government soup kitchens were feeding an incredible three million men, women, and children a day, with noticeable results. In Skibbereen, the hamlet where so many people had suffered terribly over the previous winter, the relief commissioners noted that the general health and appearance of the population had improved. Few people died during the summer months, thanks to the soup kitchens.

Over the summer, the potato plants were watched closely. When the early potatoes were harvested, there was good news. Little evidence of blight was found. With great relief, Sir Charles Trevelyan announced that the food crisis was over. He ordered the government soup kitchens to close.

Once again, the decision came too soon, for the Famine was far from over. The 1847 harvest was healthy but hopelessly small. There were not enough potatoes to sustain the Irish population over the coming winter. The laborers had two choices: either enter the workhouse or starve.

Chapter 6.

The Fever, God Bless Us and Protect Everyone

May your coffin be made of the finest wood
from a one-hundred-year-old tree
that I'll go plant tomorrow.

—TRADITIONAL IRISH BLESSING

WHEN THE IRISH POOR Law Act first established union workhouses in 1838, the institutions were designed to accommodate about one hundred thousand paupers. Before the potato crop failed in 1845, the workhouses held about thirty-eight thousand inmates. In the second year of the Famine, more than five hundred thousand people sought relief.

By 1847, the workhouse system had fallen into chaos. Many workhouses were full to overcrowded. Others had room, but they turned paupers away because they verged on bankruptcy and could not afford to buy additional food

In County Galway, the nearly bankrupt Clifden workhouse turned many people away. With no other resources, large numbers of Clifden people simply disappeared.

ILLUSTRATED LONDON NEWS, *JANUARY 5, 1850*

or supplies. This was especially true in unions where ratepayers reneged on their taxes. Many heavily indebted landlords faced bankruptcy themselves, due to the increasing rates.

Johnny Callaghan was a young boy when he worked alongside his father in the bakery of the Castlerea workhouse in County Roscommon. Each day, he saw large crowds that gathered outside the gates. Crazed with hunger, they screamed

This view gives an idea of life in the women's ward of the workhouse. The women lying in the narrow beds are probably ill. COURTESY OF THE NATIONAL LIBRARY OF IRELAND, R. 28057

and begged for food. Fearful that the people might break into the bakery, authorities attached iron bars onto the windows.

At night, before Johnny and his father walked home, they washed their hands and brushed the flour from their clothes. "My father was always nervous to appear in public with flour dust on his clothes," he said years later. "So ravenous were some people that he feared they would attack and kill him."

Heart-wrenching scenes occurred when mothers pleaded with the work-house officials to take their children. "The children are worn to skeletons," said an observer. "Women who have six or seven children beg that even two or three be taken in." Some people climbed over the gates or tried to enter by force, but they were turned out by police.

Even after admission, the inmates did not find relief, since many workhouses didn't have enough food or beds. In the Kilrush union workhouse, inmates were given a daily meal of soup and chopped turnips and sent to bed hungry. Food was so scarce at a Galway workhouse that guards carried thick sticks to keep the inmates from rushing the stirabout. In the Skibbereen workhouse, inmates slept three to a bed. They used rugs for blankets and dirty straw for bedding. "The living and the dying were stretched side by side beneath the same miserable covering," noted a visitor.

DREADED MORE THAN THE HUNGER

A person can live for months on a scanty amount of food. The starved person's body adapts by slowing its metabolism and surviving on protein, vitamins, and minerals stored in its tissues, muscles, and bones.

At first, a starving person clamors for food, but the brain slows down as the body wastes away. Some starving people were described as "cringing" and "childlike" in manner. "They will stand at a window for hours, without asking charity, giving a vacant stare, and not until driven away will they move," noted one woman. Starvation victims suffer from dehydration, hypothermia, arrhythmia, and infectons; eventually they die from heart failure, kidney failure, shock, or disease.

Without the nutritious potato, the Irish people suffered from malnutrition, which reduced their body's resistance to viruses and bacteria. It is estimated that ten times as many people died from disease than from hunger during the Famine years. The exact number will never be known, since whole families

Beggars flocked to the cities and towns to seek food or money to buy food. THACKERAY,
THE IRISH SKETCHBOOK, *LONDON: SMITH, ELDER, AND CO., 1865*

disappeared and thousands of others lie buried in unmarked graves. "If I told you where people were buried, you would not venture out at night," said one farmer from West Cork.

Diseases spread through unclean food, polluted water, and dirty living conditions. "The fever, God bless us and protect everyone, that came with the want, came, my mother used to say, from the people eating bad things," said John McCarthy. "Starving people would eat anything, even though it was decaying."

People killed and ate horses, donkeys, dogs, and cats. They even ate the carcasses of animals they found. One woman told her son how she and her hungry family had heard that their neighbor had buried two pigs. It didn't matter that the pigs had died from cholera. "I heard my mother say they hardly waited until night came," said Jimmy Quinn. "They went out and hoked up the pigs. And they took them home and they ate them . . . and damned the bit of harm it done them."

One inspector reported little food left in the south and west of Ireland. "Pigs and poultry have quite disappeared," he said. "The dogs have vanished, except here and there the ghost of one." When people died along the roadside or were buried without coffins, ravenous dogs fed on the diseased corpses. The dogs were hunted and eaten by the starving people, which further spread the diseases.

The main diseases were typhoid fever, relapsing fever, cholera, and dysentery. The infections tended to start among the poor then spread through the middle and upper middle classes. Young children and elderly adults were especially vulnerable. "The old and feeble did not stand it long," said Sean Crowley. "Death claimed them very soon. The fever took away young and old."

Both typhus and relapsing fevers were transmitted by lice. As beggars tramped the roads, looking for food and work, they carried infected lice on their bodies and clothing. At night, when a wanderer saw a hearth fire or light in a cabin, he knocked at the door, and in keeping with Irish tradition, the family invited him to spend the night. By the fire, he shared a bundle of straw or rushes for bedding.

In the crowded cabin, the lice jumped from person to person. When a louse bit a person, it passed the infected microorganism into the victim's bloodstream. If the louse was slapped, the splattered microorganism was powerful enough to enter the bloodstream through the skin. It also entered through the eyes or the lungs.

In this way, infection spread as the lice were carried from cabin to cabin. When people stood in line at the soup kitchens or gathered at the public works, the lice hopped from person to person. One person might pass the fever on to one hundred others in a single day. Within hours, the first symptoms showed in each newly infected person.

Typhus, or "black fever," was most deadly. "Black Fever was dreaded more than the hunger," said Thomas O'Flynn. "When persons were found dead in the fields or along the road, their own kith and kin denied knowing them."

Typhus attacked the small blood vessels in the skin and brain, causing the vessels to swell and block circulation. When the blood vessels became so swollen that they burst, the victim's skin turned black. "They took the black fever first between the two big toes," said Mary Nugent. "It turned black and it went up the foot and the legs and into the body. It turned as black as behind the fire till it killed them on their two feet in no time at all."

The typhus fever intensified, causing delirium to set in from the high body temperatures. Some delirious people jumped into rivers to cool off. As the disease progressed, the symptoms included vomiting, sores, gangrene, and an intolerable body odor. No cures existed for typhus. Within two weeks, the typhus victim died from heart failure.

Relapsing fever did not kill as many people as typhus, but it also caused a raging fever and vomiting. These symptoms lasted for several days, then turned to profuse sweating and extreme exhaustion. A week later, the fever and vomiting started again. The relapse occurred three or four times before the crisis ended.

Dysentery and cholera were painful diseases spread by flies and contact with polluted water. Dysentery victims suffered from nausea, shivering, fever, and

Artist James Mahony noted that he stood ankle-deep in dirt as he sketched the interior of this cabin in Skull, County Cork. A man named Mullins lies dying from fever on a heap of straw while his three children crouch over a turf fire. The man seated in the chair is probably the Vicar who tended Mullins. ILLUSTRATED LONDON NEWS, *FEBRUARY 20, 1847*

bloody diarrhea. Although not as painful as dysentery, cholera also produced profuse diarrhea, which resulted in extreme dehydration. Both diseases killed children more often than adults.

Other health problems occurred from malnutrition and vitamin deficiencies. Scurvy caused teeth to drop out and joints to swell. Hunger edema caused the abdomen to swell two or three times its normal size while legs and arms wasted away until they were as thin as pipe stems.

Children suffered worst of all from malnutrition. Many resembled little old men and women, wrinkled and bent. Their bones became so fragile and muscles so weak that they could not walk or talk. Hair fell off their heads and grew in thick downy patches on their faces. After a visit to several children's wards in workhouses, the Reverend Sidney Godolphin Osborne was moved terribly when he saw that starving children never cried or moaned, not even while dying.

Fever in the House

During the Famine, doctors did not know how to treat contagious diseases. Some of their treatments—such as the use of mercury or the cupping of patients already weakened from hunger and disease—were harmful. Since there were no cures, the best practice was prevention.

As fever outbreaks became widespread, newspapers published precautions for guarding against infection. They instructed people to clean and whitewash their houses and to move manure piles away from doorways. They told people to bathe; to wear clean, warm, and comfortable clothing; and to eat wholesome, nourishing, and moderate meals.

The hygiene instructions meant little to the Irish poor, who had sold their clothing and bedding and wore the same rags day after day. Weak from hunger and exhaustion, they could not even fetch water, let alone move manure piles.

As people learned more about the contagious nature of the diseases, they

To avoid infecting their families, some sick people went off to live and die in scalps. Relatives and neighbors left food outside. ILLUSTRATED LONDON NEWS, *5 JANUARY 1850*

avoided strangers, and the centuries-old hospitality tradition disappeared. "For the first time, the cabin doors were locked," said Shane MacCarthy, a teacher from County Cork. "A *sabh* [long stick] was drawn as a bolt inside the doors to keep out strangers or people having the sickness."

In some areas, people relied on folkways to detect the fever. "If the neighbors suspected there was any fever in a house, they used to steal up to the house at nighttime and put an onion on the windowsill," said Richard Delaney, who lived in County Wexford. "They would split the onion in two, and if the onion turned green, they knew there was fever in the house." The onion method's reliability is not known, but it was enough to warn people to stay away.

To avoid infecting their family, some people went off to live in scalps or were removed to barns and sheds. Relatives and neighbors left vessels of milk and stirabout outside the door or passed food on shovels through windows. "The mere act of touching the vessels used by the sick was supposed to bring on the sickness," said Ned Buckley.

Doctors, priests, and ministers risked their lives to tend the sick and dying. One Sligo doctor attended the sick on a daily basis, and when he didn't appear for rounds as usual one day, his nurse found him dead on the floor. "[He was] fully dressed with his feet pointed toward the door and quite dead," reported the nurse. "He was fully dressed as if ready to go to work."

Most deaths occurred in the congested slums of cities and towns. When shopkeepers and townspeople went outside in the morning, they were shocked to find bodies lying against their doors. The people had died during the night.

In some places, it became difficult to find people to bury the dead. One medical officer assured volunteers in his town that if they removed their clothes before handling the corpses and washed themselves afterward, they would not contract any diseases. It is doubtful that the practice worked, since lice leap from a dead body onto the first warm body that appears. But the men did as they were told: "They stripped themselves naked, put the corpses in coffins, and then left the coffins outside the doors," said an observer. "The corpses were buried the next day the ordinary way at the local cemetery."

Funeral traditions like the wake disappeared as the fear of contracting fever kept people away. For the Irish, there was no shame in living poor, but to be buried without a coffin was a disgrace, the ultimate sign of destitution. For coffins, people hammered old boards and barrel staves together, used drawers and pieces of furniture, and wrapped bodies in straw. Lone survivors carried the corpses on their backs to the cemetery. One mother strapped her deceased infant son in his cradle and carried him five miles to the graveyard.

SACK THEM UP

As the number of deaths increased, the British government accepted the fact that disease was epidemic. Officials acknowledged that the workhouses could not provide for the great numbers of sick people. They enacted the Irish Fever Act in April 1847.

Under the act, the government bore the cost of health care, in the form of grants that would later be repaid. The act allowed additional fever hospitals or sheds to be built beside the workhouses. It also permitted buildings to be whitewashed for sanitary purposes, the houses of sick people to be fumigated with sulphuric acid, and coffins to be supplied to those who could not otherwise afford to buy them.

People went to great lengths to obtain a workhouse coffin. A workhouse coffin was considered degrading, but less shameful than not having any at all. When Bridget Quin died, her fourteen-year-old son Tom walked three miles into Ennis to notify the relief officer and to request a workhouse coffin right away.

Tom returned home to wait with his ailing sister Mary and younger brother James. As they waited, they kept their mother's body inside the cabin, probably to keep it safe from wild dogs. Three more days passed, bringing more tragedy.

A body is removed from a Skibbereen cabin. LORD DUFFERIN AND THE HONORABLE G. F. BOYLE, NARRATIVE OF A JOURNEY FROM OXFORD TO SKIBBEREEN; *COURTESY OF THE NATIONAL LIBRARY OF IRELAND, R. 27063*

Mary's condition worsened, and she died. "We had not a halfpenny to buy a candle," Tom said. "We watched at night to keep off the rats."

Finally, eight days after his mother's death, the authorities arrived. When the emaciated and squalid-looking boys emerged from the cabin, a witness said, "They presented such a horrible spectacle that it would be vain to attempt a description." Tom Quin and his twelve-year-old brother James were admitted to the Ennis workhouse.

The tragedy was reported in the local newspaper, and a number of investigations followed. Although the coroner's jury blamed the relieving officer for negligence, the Ennis Board of Guardians absolved the officer of any responsibility.

In County Mayo Thomas O'Flynn recalled the man whose job was to convey the sick to the workhouse. "He had the only horse and cart . . . [and] was paid so much per head," said Thomas. "The patient was put in a sack, feet first, and the sack was tied closely around the neck and labelled. Up to seven or eight patients were laid out in the cart, which was then set off on its cogglesome journey to the workhouse. Few ever returned. . . . The contractor received the name 'Sack Them Up' from putting the patients in the sack."

Some sick people entered the workhouse, hoping for a decent burial after they died. Many were disappointed to learn that they would be buried unceremoniously in a large pit, without even the blessing of a priest. "When a person was near death," said Johnny Callaghan, "he or she was removed from other parts of the workhouse to a large room at the gable-end. . . . From the window, there were a few boards slanting down to the earth and beneath was a huge grave or pit. The corpse was slid down the boards into the pit and lime was put over the corpse." Some burial pits held as many as nine hundred bodies.

In some fever hospitals and workhouses, workers carted the dead to the graveyard in "bottomless coffins." These coffins were specially constructed with hinged bottoms. When the worker pulled the release, the coffin bottom opened like a door, allowing the corpse to drop into the grave. This way, one coffin was used many times.

Because the dead were buried immediately, grim stories circulated about people buried alive. "Tom Gearins was a young lad at the time of the Famine," said Margaret Donovan, from County Cork. "With many others, he was taken and thrown into the Famine Hole in Skibbereen Alley. He was not dead, and somehow he was able to raise his hand." Tom was rescued, but both his legs had been broken in the fall. After that, it was said that Tom "arose from the dead."

Another story circulated about a Carlow undertaker who earned an unsavory reputation. "He collected people before they were quite dead," said James Doyle. "One man woke up as he was being carried in a hinge-bottomed coffin for burial. He shouted to know where he was, and the undertaker replied, 'We are going to bury you.' 'How'll you bury me when I'm not dead,' said the man. The undertaker calmly replied, 'Oh, the drop will kill you anyhow.'"

ᕲᐤ Chapter 7.

A Terrible Leveling of Houses

I am a houseless outcast; I have neither bed nor board,
Nor living things to look upon; nor comfort save the Lord.
—FROM THE BALLAD "WILLY GUILLIAND" BY SAMUEL FERGUSON,
CIRCA 1850

O N A COLD DAMP NOVEMBER day, several rough-looking men rode up to a cluster of small cabins not far from the seaside town of Kilrush, County Clare. Inside one of the cabins, a thirty-year-old woman named Bridget O'Donnel lay on a bed of straw. She was seven months' pregnant with her fourth child and sick with fever.

When Bridget heard the men outside, she knew right away what they wanted, even before they pounded on the door and called out to her to give up

Bridget O'Donnel is shown here with her two surviving children. ILLUSTRATED LONDON NEWS, *DECEMBER 22, 1849*

The roof has been torn off and the family evicted from this cabin. ILLUSTRATED LONDON NEWS, *JANUARY 5, 1850*

the cabin. "Dan Sheedy and five or six men came to tumble my house," said Bridget. "They wanted me to give possession."

Stubbornly, Bridget refused to leave her bed. "I had a fever," she said, "and was within two months of my down-lying [giving birth]."

It didn't matter to the men that Bridget O'Donnel was pregnant and sick. They had orders to follow. When she refused to come out, they battered in the cabin door. One man climbed onto the roof, pulled away the thatch, and attached a rope to the main beam. Other men pulled at the rope to bring down the cabin walls. "[They] had half of it knocked down when two neighbors, women, carried me out," said Bridget.

Fearing the worst for Bridget and her unborn baby, neighbors carried her into their cabin and sent for the priest, who administered last rites. Eight days after the eviction, Bridget gave birth seven weeks prematurely to a stillborn baby. Several days later, her thirteen-year-old son died from fever. Bridget and her two daughters were admitted to the Kilrush union workhouse.

CRUEL, HEARTLESS WORK

As more small farmers and laborers grew unable to pay their rent, the landlords found their incomes reduced drastically. At the same time, the landlords' expenses were skyrocketing, as they were expected to pay for the workhouses and public works. The heaviest financial burden fell on unions where the food crisis was greatest, since more people in those areas needed relief.

Many landlords, heavily in debt, couldn't afford to pay the high rates. They grew fearful of losing their property. The British government insisted that rates had to be collected, by force if necessary. "Arrest, remand, do anything you can," ordered one British leader. "Send horse, foot, and dragoons, all the world will applaud you."

In June 1847 a frustrated Galway landlord named William Gregory proposed an amendment to save ratepayers money. The amendment, known as the Quarter Acre or Gregory Clause, denied government relief to any tenant and his family who rented more than one-quarter of an acre. To enter a workhouse or fever hospital, such tenants had to relinquish their cabin and land. The law also enabled landlords to evict tenants who rented less than one-quarter acre.

Many landlords were eager to clear their estates of residents who couldn't pay their rent. For the landlord, fewer tenants meant fewer rates to pay. It also meant that land could be converted to pastureland for dairy and livestock farming, a

In County Clare, nearly the entire village of Moveen was evicted

a few days before Christmas. ILLUSTRATED LONDON NEWS, *DECEMBER 22, 1849*

more profitable and less problematic business than renting property to tenants. "The idle houses were razed to the ground," said Sean O'Dunleavy, "the fences levelled, and large regular fields from fifty to seventy acres took their place. The stones of the tenants' houses were used for building." From the altar, priests shamed the landlords who evicted tenants. They wrote letters to newspapers, denouncing their actions.

Not all landlords were heartless. Several reduced the rents or renounced rents altogether. "My grandfather, God rest his soul, went to pay his rent to the landlord," said Séamus Reardon. "But the landlord told him, 'Feed your family first, then give me what you can afford when times get better.'"

But many landlords felt that they had the right to make a profit, even if it meant evicting tenants. For these men, it became a case of either evict or be evicted. If they wanted to keep their estates, they had to rid themselves of tenants and find a more profitable source of income. Determined to save their property, the landlords alerted the sheriff and filled out the paperwork. "It was cruel, heartless work," said Ned Buckley. "But it was usual in those days."

Eviction Day

On eviction day, the sheriff and his men took crowbars to the house. Often British soldiers went along, armed with bayonets and muskets. "One spring morning the townland was full of redcoat soldiers," said Sean Crowley, speaking about the day his grandfather's family was evicted. "Before the sun was down that evening, every tenant on that townland was homeless."

The sheriff stood outside the cabin and called out the tenant's name, saying something like, "Bridget O'Donnel, I hereby order you to give up your house." If the tenant refused, the cabin doors were battered in and every family member was dragged out, no matter the circumstances.

Little mattered except the landlord's orders. Like Bridget, one man was evicted even though he was sick. "He was brought out and laid under a shed,

On eviction day, a family pleads with the sheriff, but he has orders to follow. Soldiers stand by, ready to use force if necessary. ILLUSTRATED LONDON NEWS, DECEMBER 16, 1848

covered with turf, and his house thrown down," said a neighbor. In another village, the bailiff took the roof off his own brother's house while the brother and his family were still inside.

After the cabin was collapsed, the thatched roof was set on fire. In one townland, the landlord offered money to any man who would set fire to the tumbled house. To his surprise, the evicted tenant himself, named Diver, agreed to do it.

Some families were tricked into believing that the local workhouse would take them in, if they surrendered their cabins, but the overcrowded workhouses turned them away. With nowhere else to go, this homeless family found shelter in a scalp.

ILLUSTRATED LONDON NEWS, *DECEMBER 16, 1848*

"Diver stepped into the kitchen, where some turf was still smouldering on the hearth and brought them out on a shovel," said an eyewitness, who watched incredulously. "He climbed onto the roof and placed the embers among the thatch. In a few moments, it was ablaze, and in a short time his home was gone." The tenant then pocketed the landlord's money, nodded to his neighbors, turned on his heel, and walked away.

Police records show that evictions increased drastically after the Gregory Clause was passed. Over a six-year period, at least 250,000 people lost their homes, with the greatest number occurring in Kilrush union, where Bridget O'Donnel lived. The exact number will never be known, since many tenants peaceably surrendered their homes and others were evicted illegally.

A large number of evictions also took place in County Mayo. Ten days before Christmas, the magistrate evicted the inhabitants of three villages with the help of troops. The bewildered tenants stood in the rain and watched as the soldiers tore the roofs off their cabins and battered down the walls. "It was a night of high wind and storm," said an elderly woman. "But the wailing could be heard at a great distance." The evicted families built makeshift shelters out of wood and straw, but the soldiers were ordered to drive them out.

Jim Killian had paid his rent in full, but he was still evicted. For shelter, he cut a few trees and built a scalp on the spot that had once been the family garden. When police discovered the shelter, they arrested him, and he was sentenced to a two-month jail term for destroying the landlord's trees.

Some agents threatened the other tenants, warning them not to take in evicted families. When the notorious female agent Bess Rice turned out Sean Connors and his nine-month-old daughter, no one dared to help them. Sean found a large outcrop of rock and tacked a few wool sacks against the outside for protection from wind and rain. Eventually, he and his daughter found a place to live in another townland. According to legend, after Bess Rice died, a descendent of the Connors family played his hornpipe as he danced on her grave.

This woman shakes her fists as she stands in front of her tumbled house. After an eviction, some women threw ashes from their hearth into the nearest river and called down curses upon the landlord and his men. ILLUSTRATED LONDON NEWS, DECEMBER 22, 1849

Years later, Captain Arthur Kennedy, the Poor Law inspector for Kilrush union, was still haunted by the evictions he had seen. "I can tell you that there were days in that western county when I came back from some scene of eviction so maddened by the sights of hunger and misery I had seen in a day's work, that I felt disposed to take the gun from behind the door and shoot the first landlord I met."

TURN THEM OUT

A small number of landlords participated in a scheme called "landlord-assisted emigration." These landlords evicted their tenants and paid their passage to the United States or Canada. Some even chartered ships to transport them. Landlords found it cheaper to export the destitute than to maintain them for one year in the union workhouse. Assisted emigration offered a cheap solution to the problem of overcrowded workhouses, overpopulation on estates, and the high rates.

At first, people praised the landlords for their generosity. After all, no law required them to pay their tenants' passage to a new country. Many people believed that the tenants would be better off abroad than at home. But public opinion about assisted emigration changed as people realized that tenants were forced to leave: tenants had no choice when they were surrounded by bailiffs and soldiers. Penniless and struggling to keep their families alive, tenants were in no position to refuse any offer. "The tenants had to pay their rent or leave," said Charles Clarke. "So they left."

Though most tenants surrendered their homes peaceably, some retaliated against their landlords. In the late spring of 1847, Major Dennis Mahon evicted over eight hundred laborers from his Strokestown estate in County Roscommon and offered them free passage to Canada, which they accepted. He chartered two ships and provided extra provisions for their journey.

Some people feel that Mahon acted generously, but others claim that he sought the cheapest—and therefore least seaworthy—vessels. During the voyage, typhus and relapsing fevers—known as "ship fever" at sea—broke out, killing many passengers. It is estimated that 25 percent of Mahon's tenants died on the voyage. When the ships eventually arrived in Quebec, the survivors were wretched and diseased.

Back home, Major Mahon continued to evict, and he served eviction notices to three thousand more tenants, including eighty-four widows. He offered them passage to Canada, but the tenants refused. "[They] would neither pay nor go," said one man. Frustrated, Mahon called them troublemakers. "These tenants I should be glad to get rid of on any terms," he said.

Over the summer, whispers of "tyrant" circulated among the people. In November, as Mahon traveled home from a meeting in an open carriage one evening, two men ambushed him and shot him in the chest. It didn't take long for word about his death to spread. The next night, for miles around, bonfires burned in celebration on the hilltops.

Dennis Mahon wasn't the only landlord to be attacked: seven landlords and ten other men were ambushed and shot that fall and winter. All but one died. "I never knew them [the tenants] to attack anyone for money," said one Tipperary merchant. "But touch the farm and turn them out and they get wild and frantic."

British leaders grew convinced that the murders were part of an organized tenant rebellion. To prevent further unrest Parliament passed the Crime and Outrage Bill in December 1847. The bill provided additional police protection and power, and it restricted the right of the Irish people to carry firearms. In a show of force, fifteen thousand British troops were sent into Ireland.

Though authorities worried that the laborers were arming themselves, their fears seem unfounded. Most laborers didn't have money for guns. They were dying from hunger and disease, their cabins were being demolished, and the workhouses were turning them away. Any laborers fortunate enough to have money were spending it on food—or on passage out of Ireland.

The Going Away

May the road rise to meet you,
May the wind be always at your back,
May the sun shine warm upon your face,
And rains fall soft upon your fields,
And until we meet again,
May God hold you in the hollow of His hand.

— TRADITIONAL IRISH BLESSING

T HE IRISH HAD BEGUN to emigrate to the United States and Canada many years before the potato blight struck. But they had never left in large numbers, the way they did during the Famine. "That was the time the 'going away' started," said Joseph Dougherty. "They left in crowds." Nearly two million people fled Ireland during the Famine years and the years that immediately followed.

In Cork, the quays were crowded with emigrants anxious to leave Ireland. Within one eight-day period, eleven ships carrying 1,568 passengers sailed from the single port of Cork. ILLUSTRATED LONDON NEWS, *MAY 10, 1851*

Some emigrants put aside money for years, living in rags and squalor until they had saved enough to purchase passage tickets. Others were funded by landlords, the British government, or charities. Most were aided by family already in the United States. Nearly one million pounds sterling, in small drafts ranging from two to ten pounds (about ten to fifty dollars), was sent from the United States annually.

THE AMERICAN WAKE

Brokerage firms soon realized that emigration meant profit. By 1847, brokerage firms from Liverpool, England, had established themselves in nearly every Irish town. They posted handbills and advertisements on trees and shops and in nearly every public place. The handbills promised plenty of work and high wages for men and women in America. The advertisements offered comfortable passage, good service, and economical fares, ranging from two to five pounds (about ten to twenty-five dollars) on a variety of sailing packets.

The promises sounded good to the Irish people. Though many sailed directly for American ports, vast numbers took advantage of cheaper fares to the British territory of Canada, then headed for the United States border as soon as possible. Three out of every four Famine emigrants settled in the United States, about one and one-half million in all.

Most emigrants left in spring or early summer, to avoid crossing the Atlantic Ocean during the risky winter months. Once families decided to emigrate, they desired to get away as soon as possible. Some slipped away in the middle of the night, out of fear that their landlord would stop them, especially if rent was owed. "He might take from them money and everything else they had, and so their last state would be worst than their first," explained Jane O'Kane. "They would have nothing at home to live on and not have the wherewithal to emigrate."

Most emigrants had little to pack, perhaps bedding and a few meager food provisions. "Each person brought a supply of oaten cakes, baked three times," said Jane O'Kane. "[They were] baked in the ordinary way first, then allowed to cool, then baked again until each large cake was hard as stone." When available, some people also took salted herring, potatoes, and oatmeal.

Some emigrants prepared a special "frog bread," made from a mixture of oatmeal and the ashes of a roasted frog. They believed the bread protected seafarers from the deadly ship fever. Emigrants also carried a "caul," the membrane that encloses a human fetus before birth, to protect them from drowning. Many

Family and friends gathered to say goodbye. The guests danced, drank, sang . . . and cried. ILLUSTRATED LONDON NEWS, *DECEMBER 30, 1848*

emigrants took along a chunk of the "auld sod," or turf, as a memory of Ireland.

The night before the emigrant's departure, friends and family held an "American wake," which grew out of Irish funeral traditions. The wake made sense, since no one expected the emigrant to return and many feared they would never see their loved ones again. During the wake, family and friends prayed the rosary, ate, drank, sang, danced, and played games. No amount of merriment could hide the sadness families felt, especially when they said goodbye to their children. At one wake, when a father asked his departing son to dance, saying, "Get up here, son, and face me in a step, for likely it will be the last step ever we'll dance," there wasn't a dry eye in the house.

The next morning, the priest gave a final blessing, and family and friends accompanied the traveler as far as possible. "[My father] walked forty miles on the occasion of his uncle's departure for Canada," said Connor O'Neill. "The banks of the Shannon used to be lined with people, and the sights witnessed would break your heart."

In 1848 Diarmuid O'Donovan Rossa, now seventeen, saw his family broken up and scattered. His father had died the spring before, then his family was evicted from their home. Diarmuid found work in nearby Skibbereen, but his widowed mother, two brothers, and sister decided to emigrate, leaving him alone in Ireland. "I suppose they thought I was old enough to take care of myself," said Diarmuid.

To see them off, Diarmuid walked as far as the crossroads leading to the Cove of Cork. "The cry of the weeping and wailing of that day rings in my ears still," he recalled years later.

THE VOYAGE

Many emigrants had never traveled so far from their village. Some had never seen a city, a ship, or the sea. For anyone who had just left a mud cabin with one tiny window and a clay floor, the sights and sounds of the port city were wondrous. Perhaps the most incredible sight was the docks laden with food—pork, butter, oats, eggs, sides of ham and beef—all intended for export to English markets.

The emigrants purchased passage from ticket brokers. Dishonest ticket brokers and greedy ship owners found it easy to cheat naive emigrants. Some sold

On the morning of departure, this emigrant's long journey to America begins with a blessing from the priest. ILLUSTRATED LONDON NEWS, *MAY 10, 1851*

bogus tickets for ships that didn't exist or oversold the steerage space, leaving ticket holders out of luck once the steerage was full. Emigrants also had to beware of fast-talking strangers who tried to sell them useless items like compasses, which they would not need on their journey. Eventually, shipping regulations improved.

Once emigrants bought their passage tickets, they stayed in lodging houses

Family and friends accompanied the emigrant as far as possible. Here, they watch as the ship departs from the dock quay in Galway. ILLUSTRATED LONDON NEWS, *JUNE 8, 1850*

until the sailing date. "The boat would not leave the dock until the wind and weather were favourable," said Jane O'Kane. "One young man was held up in Sligo for three weeks. His parents brought down fresh supplies of food each weekend. They wanted him to return home, but he would not because, he said, everybody would laugh at him if he did."

When the sailing day arrived, the emigrants carried their belongings and

A mother and her children sit with their belongings. Their trunk is labeled JACK SULLIVAN *and* GOIN TO AMERIKY. ILLUSTRATED LONDON NEWS, *MAY 10, 1851*

dragged their bedding, perhaps a feather tick or trusses of straw, down to the dock. Before boarding, they underwent a hurried medical examination. Some doctors simply sat behind a window and looked at the passengers' tongues as they walked past. "Many appeared to be quite unfit to undergo the hardship of a long voyage," remarked one man. "But they were inspected and passed by a doctor."

Most emigrants traveled as steerage passengers, having purchased the cheapest fare. To reach the steerage section, they climbed down to the deepest hold of the ship, lit only by lanterns. Passengers slept side by side on narrow wooden berths, with no room to turn over. For women, water closets, or toilets, were located at either end of the steerage section; men went above deck.

Before iron-hulled steamships were introduced in 1850, sailing ships took about forty days to cross the Atlantic Ocean. In poor weather, the crossing took much longer. To escape the foul-smelling hold, steerage passengers stayed on deck as much as possible. During storms, they were forced below and the hatches were battened down. The hold felt suffocating and ominous as the sea seeped in and timbers creaked.

By law, ships were required to provide each passenger with food and water. Each adult received one pound of bread, flour, rice, oatmeal, or potatoes each day, which they cooked over fires on the afterdeck. They were also allotted three quarts of water each day to drink, wash, and cook. By today's standards, the daily food ration totals one loaf of bread or five or six medium potatoes—barely enough to keep a person from starving. Children under fourteen were given half-rations.

To pass the time, passengers played games, sang, and danced between the decks, and the older children hunted rats. The long voyage frayed nerves, and passengers grew quarrelsome, often bickering as they cooked their stirabout and oaten cakes. "The quarrels only ended at seven when Jack in the Shrouds [a young seaman] poured water on the fire," noted Robert Whyte, a cabin-class passenger. "Then the squabbling group snatched up their pots and pans and half-blinded by steam, they descended into the hold with their half-cooked supper."

As the voyage progressed, water and food rations ran short. Each day, the ship's crew eked out provisions to make them last and added larger doses of vinegar to the water barrels. The acetic acid in the vinegar probably slowed the growth of bacteria.

THE COFFIN SHIPS

American and British governments enacted various Passenger Acts, designed to regulate the shipping trade and to protect passengers. The acts were difficult to enforce, especially in small harbors that lacked government supervision.

Before boarding the ship, emigrants underwent a rudimentary medical examination. In some families, the strongest members emigrated and the weakest stayed behind.
ILLUSTRATED LONDON NEWS, *JULY 6, 1850*

This greatly jeopardized the emigrants' safety and welfare, since greedy ship captains and owners wanted to make as much money as possible and landlords wanted the cheapest fares possible for their tenants.

By law, ships were required to limit the number of passengers. American ships could carry no more than two people for every five tons of the vessels' registered tonnage; British ships allowed three people for every five tons. Without

This crowded steerage section will be the emigrants' home for the next forty days or more. The wooden berths allowed eighteen inches in width for each adult passenger and nine inches for each child. ILLUSTRATED LONDON NEWS, *MAY 10, 1851*

proper supervision, overcrowded ships often sailed, carrying twice the legal number of passengers, with no doctor or proper medical supplies and too few provisions of food and water. "The poor people were packed like cattle into sailing vessels and badly fed while at sea," said John Phillips.

The medical inspections did not protect passengers from sickness and disease. Since passengers had little means to wash themselves and their clothing and bedding, body lice spread quickly, transmitting ship fever. Diarrhea and dysentery also resulted from inadequately cooked food and putrid drinking water. When people died, their bodies were sewn into canvas shrouds and buried at sea. Some emigrants claimed that hungry sharks followed the ships, waiting for the splash of bodies.

The worst conditions existed on ships sailing to Canada. So many passengers died that these ships became known as "coffin ships." One ship, the *Elizabeth and Sarah*, violated nearly every Passenger Act. The seventy-six-year-old ship carried 126 passengers above her legal limit. The ship had thirty-two hastily constructed berths in the hold, forcing most steerage passengers to sleep on the floor. Buckets were used for toilets. The ship should have carried 12,532 gallons of water but had only 8,700 gallons in leaky casks. The captain never distributed the food provisions. The ship took eight weeks to reach Quebec; forty-two passengers died during the voyage.

Stories about the *Elizabeth and Sarah* and other coffin ships reached home: the *Larch*, which buried 108 of her 440 passengers at sea and arrived at Grosse Isle, Canada, with 150 more stricken with fever; the captain of the overcrowded *Amelia Mary*, who abandoned seventeen passengers on a desolate Irish beach to avoid a large fine; the *Ocean Monarch*, which caught fire twenty-five miles out of Liverpool, England, burned for twelve hours, then sank in sixty feet of water; the *Hannah*, whose captain and crew grabbed the lifeboat and abandoned the emigrants after the ship struck an iceberg. Sixty passengers died when the ship sank forty minutes later. A passing ship rescued 129 others who had clambered onto the ice.

The horror continued after the ships reached Canada. To prevent the spread of disease in Canada, ships underwent an inspection at a quarantine station located on Grosse Isle, an island lying in the middle of the Saint Lawrence River. Sick passengers disembarked and entered the quarantine hospital for treatment and recovery, and the ships were washed down with disinfectant.

To pass the time and fight off homesickness, emigrants played games, sang, and danced between the decks. ILLUSTRATED LONDON NEWS, *JULY 6, 1850*

Under ordinary circumstances, this system worked. But the large influx of Irish emigrants overwhelmed the inspection officials. At one point during the spring of 1847, forty ships waited in a line two miles long down the Saint Lawrence River. The ships held about fourteen thousand emigrants, many stricken with fever and dysentery. To make matters worse, immigration officials expected forty-five thousand more emigrants to arrive later that year.

It was a nightmare. Inspection officials could not process the emigrants quickly enough, and disease spread as passengers were quarantined together for days. After inspecting one emigrant ship, a medical officer commented: "I have seen a stream of foul air issuing from the hatches as dense and palpable as seen on a foggy day from a dung heap."

When the sick passengers were finally ferried ashore, they were simply deposited on the beach. A horrified priest remarked, "They were lying on the beach, crawling on the mud, and dying like fish out of water."

Tents and sheds were erected as hospitals, but they lacked beds, supplies, and equipment. Bedding became soaked on the damp ground. Hastily built sheds had no privies, and with so many emigrants suffering from dysentery, human filth lay everywhere. "I have known many poor families prefer to burrow under heaps of loose stones, near the shore, rather than accept the shelter," said one man.

Sixteen-year-old Tom Flynn, the young man who fled Ireland after he poisoned his landlord's fish, was luckier than many. He found work in Canada, saved his money, and sent passage for his widowed mother and brothers and sisters. When they arrived, their ship was quarantined in the harbor. Unable to wait, Tom borrowed a rowboat and rowed out to the ship. He located his family, sneaked them off the ship, and hid them beneath a covering in the bottom of the rowboat.

As Tom started back to shore, he was spotted by a British guard. "What have ye there?" shouted the guard. Tom boldly replied, "Fish, do you want some?"

Winter proved a risky time to cross the Atlantic Ocean. A hard gale tossed the Edmund *wildly, tearing the canvas to shreds and snapping two masts; then the ship was dashed broadside against rocks. Ninety-six passengers drowned; the remaining one hundred ten managed to scramble to safety onto the rocks.* ILLUSTRATED LONDON NEWS, DECEMBER 7, 1850

The guard shouted back, "No, just keep away from here!" "And Tom gladly did," said his granddaughter, who related the story.

By the end of 1847, about one hundred thousand emigrants in all had headed to Canada. Nearly twenty thousand emigrants died, either in the crossing, in the hastily erected hospitals, or in the nearby towns. Orphaned children were adopted or sent to live in orphanages. According to some estimates, as many as 17 percent of the Famine emigrants died soon after reaching North America.

ORPHAN EMIGRATION SCHEME

Not all Famine refugees headed for Canada and the United States. About three hundred thousand Irish emigrants booked passage to England, a day's sail across the Irish Sea. Most did not intend to stay in England. They planned to earn money and continue west to America from there or travel east to the continent of Europe.

Australia was begging for settlers, especially women, since most emigrants were men. Because fare to Australia cost four times more than to North America, most Irish could not afford passage. The Australian authorities and government devised a plan to sponsor willing emigrants, and nearly fourteen thousand Irish people took advantage of the assisted emigration. This number included orphaned girls, between the ages of fourteen and eighteen, who were inmates in the workhouses.

Many female orphans were eager to emigrate, especially those who hoped to find husbands after they landed. The first ships carried 2,219 female orphans from eighty-eight unions. They were given new clothes, hats, boots, and a comb for the journey. They were lectured on passage at the depot, and they received medical examinations and inoculations. While at sea, their diet and accommodations were superior to that of other vessels. A matron watched over the girls and teachers taught them reading and writing.

Though initial reports claimed that some girls misbehaved during the voyage, others described the girls as orderly, obedient, and hard-working. Upon arrival, the girls faced some ethnic prejudice, but many Australian employers were impressed by their "good conduct." Within two weeks, every girl was employed. When the emigration scheme ended in May 1850, more than four thousand Irish girls had emigrated from 118 workhouses.

No Irish Need Apply

No disaster comparable to Grosse Isle took place in the United States, but Irish emigrants faced other problems. As long as the starving Irish stayed in Ireland, the Americans seemed sympathetic: they organized relief plans and sent money, food, and clothing overseas.

Once the Irish landed in America, the sympathetic feelings disappeared. Americans feared the destitute, emaciated emigrants, many so weakened from hunger and disease that they could not work. The Americans also feared the spread of typhus and other infectious diseases. They also worried that the newcomers would take jobs away from them and drag down wages. To prevent this, many employers refused to hire the Irish. They put signs in their windows and advertisements in newspapers that read "NINA," meaning "no Irish need apply."

To prevent the Irish emigrants from becoming a financial burden on American taxpayers, the United States Congress acted quickly to enforce the Passenger Acts. In 1847 Congress reduced the number of passengers allowed per American ship, which raised the minimum cost of passage and further restricted emigration. Inspecting officers also refused ships whose passengers were too sick and too weak to work. Forced to turn back to sea, most ships headed to Canada. Since Canada was a British territory, inspection officials could not refuse ships from Britain or Ireland.

But the Irish did not give up. Emigrants like Tom Flynn were determined

This emigrant ship is bound for Australia. The British government and Australian authorities organized a scheme to sponsor emigrants. ILLUSTRATED LONDON NEWS, JULY 20, 1840

to succeed. Though Tom first landed in Canada, he made his way to the United States, where he accepted any job, no matter how difficult, dangerous, or dirty. "[He] worked in lumber camps, on building railroads, an expert river man driving logs, and in the granite quarries in Maine and New Hampshire," said his granddaughter, Elizabeth. "He became an American citizen in 1856. He voted for Abraham Lincoln in 1860."

The Irish soon formed a large percentage of the American labor force. Like Tom Flynn, they worked at the lowest jobs, digging canals, railways, and roads. They worked in factories, mills, and coal mines. They worked for the lowest wages—often as little as fifty cents per day. For any worker who had earned eight pence a day—about sixteen cents—on the public works in Ireland, the new wages seemed enormous.

THE STATE OF IRELAND

As the emigration craze swept over Ireland, entire villages and small towns became deserted. British leaders were not alarmed at the high emigration rate, and it's likely they were glad to see them go. They were more troubled by recent events in Europe. In France, the working people had overthrown the king and established a republic. In Austria, the people had forced their leading statesman to leave the country, which led to further uprisings against Austrian rule. Revolts had also broken out in several German and Italian states.

By April 1848, British leaders feared more than ever that Ireland was ripe for rebellion. In a letter to Lord John Russell, Queen Victoria admitted: "The state of Ireland is most alarming and most anxious; altogether there is so much inflammable matter all around us that it makes one tremble."

෧‍ඏ Chapter 9.

Where Would the War Begin?

If you be too harsh, you will be broken,
If you be too feeble, you will be crushed.

—CORMAC MAC AIRT, A.D. 267, "INSTRUCTION OF A KING"

IN A STONE FARMHOUSE, not far from the hillside village of Ballingarry in County Tipperary, a young widowed mother lived with her seven children. During the summer of 1848, Widow McCormack heard rumblings about a possible uprising against the British, but she didn't pay much attention. She had heard such talk before, and even though she often wondered if war might break out, she felt certain that it would not begin in Ballingarry.

In July the uprising talk grew louder among the Ballingarry people. Some laborers cut ash trees, fashioned the wood into smoothly hewn handles, and forged sharp pikes at the blacksmith's shop. Others counted shots for their

In preparation for the rebellion, the blacksmith hammered iron into spearlike tips for the laborers' pikes. ILLUSTRATED LONDON NEWS, *AUGUST 5, 1848*

fowling pieces and pistols. Some readied themselves with scythes and pitchforks. During the last days of July, the small rebel army, about two hundred in all, paraded and drilled in the Ballingarry streets. They longed for the chance to fight the British, fair and square.

On Saturday, July 29, the rebels received word that a police column was approaching their village. Excited, they prepared to defend Ballingarry. They threw up a hasty barricade of carts and timber, took their positions, and waited for the attack to begin.

The Widow McCormack lived with her seven children in this two-story stone farmhouse, a short distance outside Ballingarry, County Tipperary. ILLUSTRATED LONDON NEWS, *AUGUST 5, 1848*

KATTY, WILL THEY KILL US?

The troubling news reached Widow McCormack. She grew concerned for the safety of her two oldest children at school, and she decided that they would be safer at home. She pulled her black bonnet over her head, tied its strings beneath her chin, and told ten-year-old Katty to mind her four younger brothers and sisters while she was gone. The widow promised to return shortly, then hurried out the front gate and started toward the national schoolhouse.

Katty's mother had been gone a short while when Katty heard a commotion outside. She dashed to the window, and in the distance, she spotted about forty uniformed policemen running through the pasture and hedge, scrambling over walls and ditches. They were chased by an angry mob of men and women. Most carried pikes, pitchforks, and scythes. Several had guns.

The police reached the stone wall surrounding the McCormack farmhouse. A man on horseback, Inspector Tom Trant, shouted for them to take cover inside the house. The men rushed over the stone wall, through the McCormacks' cabbage patch, and burst inside the house. "We all set up a cry when the police came in," Katty later told a newspaper reporter. "But they told us to be quiet."

Inspector Trant ordered the men to barricade the windows and doors. The children watched as the policemen ripped doors from hinges and shoved furniture into place. Several men broke into Widow McCormack's bedroom and pushed her feather bed and mattress against the front door.

Katty hurried her brothers and sisters into the kitchen, where they huddled near the hearth. Little Maggy, age two and one-half, crept between Katty and her brother Wat. The little girl buried her head in her sister's lap and whimpered, "Katty, will they kill us?"

At that moment, stones crashed through the kitchen window, shattering the glass. A gun fired, and a musket ball burst through the shutters, splintering the wood. "The ball struck the chimney close above where the cat was asleep," said Katty. "It knocked down soot and she jumped and ran. We never saw her for three days after that." In the barnyard, the animals turned wild with fright. "The mare and her foal and the cow and calves all ran about as if mad," Katty added.

The police knocked portholes in the farmhouse walls and fired back at the rebels. Hearing the gun blasts, the children jumped up and ran into the hall, near the front door. "I screamed and Wat screamed, and Johnny and Ellen and Maggy," said Katty. "They cried to me and Wat not to let them be killed, for the guns inside and out were like thunder."

A policeman grabbed the children and pushed them to safety in a large closet beneath the staircase. He ordered them to be quiet, then continued to shoot from behind the door. "Every time he fired out, the flash of his gun made all the place we lay in light," said Katty. "When he went to load, he turned the one end of the gun against my foot."

To the McCormack children huddled beneath the staircase, it seemed as though war had broken out. Katty's family had often speculated about war in Ireland. "We used to say, my aunts and my mother and grandfather, where would the war begin?" said Katty. "But we never thought of all places in Ireland, it would be at our house it would begin."

Little did Katty know: plans for an uprising had begun months earlier.

Young Ireland

The spring of 1848 had been cold, but faith in the potato had been restored. Little blight had been found in the 1847 harvest, and the Irish believed that the blight was over at last.

Enthusiastic farmers planted seed potatoes everywhere—in fields, in bogs, and on rocky hillsides. Small farmers strained to find money to buy seed, selling their last pieces of furniture and clothing. Overall, farmers and laborers planted three times as many potatoes as they had the previous year. The Irish felt so confident, they planted few green crops such as cabbages, beans, carrots, and kale.

Sunshine was plentiful throughout May and June, and as the plants sprouted, landlords and large farmers looked forward to collecting enough rent to pay off their debts. Small farmers and laborers looked forward to having enough to eat for the first time in three years.

While the hopeful Irish planted their seed potatoes, a revolutionary spirit was growing among members of a militant group known as Young Ireland. They were inspired by recent rebellions in Europe.

For the most part, members of Young Ireland shared a dream similar to the people in France, Austria, and the German and Italian states. Like their European countrymen, they felt pride in their history and culture. They hungered for independence and reform that would guarantee their rights and freedoms. They longed for home rule and the opportunity to govern themselves. For Young Ireland, self-government meant abolishing the Act of Union, restoring the Irish Parliament in Dublin, and sweeping the British from Ireland.

The Young Ireland leaders came from diverse backgrounds. They were men like William Smith O'Brien, a Protestant-Irish landlord; Terrence McManus, a prosperous young merchant; James Fintan Lalor, a poor, hunchbacked farmer; Thomas Francis Meagher, the son of the Catholic mayor of Waterford; John Mitchel, the son of a Presbyterian minister; and Charles Gavan Duffy, a newspaper editor and son of a Catholic grocer.

To set their plan in motion, Young Ireland formed revolutionary clubs all over Ireland and recruited members. The members were as diverse as their leaders. They came from the middle and upper classes. They were Protestants and Catholics, farmers, young lawyers, journalists, merchants, and even landlords. Like their leaders, many were intellectuals, people who believed that problems could be solved through reason.

At the Young Ireland meetings, the leaders made speeches and discussed ways to save the Irish people from hunger, poverty, and eviction. Most agreed that the land system had to change, but the leaders could not agree on the best means to accomplish this. James Fintan Lalor argued for peaceful change, achieved through a general rent strike. John Mitchel called for an armed uprising and published instructions on street fighting in his newspaper. William Smith O'Brien and Charles Gavan Duffy believed that landlords and tenants weren't enemies but natural partners who needed to cooperate.

In March 1848, O'Brien and several others traveled to Paris. They met with the new French president, Lamartine, and asked him if France would support Ireland in a fight for freedom. Unbeknown to the Irish leaders, the British government had sent a stern warning to the French, telling them that France should not interfere with Britain's internal affairs.

Lamartine heeded the warning. Politely but firmly, he refused to help Ireland. As the disappointed Irishmen left France, a group of women gave them a green, white, and orange banner. The tricolored banner would have great significance in years to come.

The men returned home and continued their activities. The British government grew more anxious that the laborers might rebel, just as the working classes had rebelled in Europe. The British knew conditions had never been worse for the Irish laborers. In 1848 Irish poverty existed to a greater extent than ever before. More beggars crowded the city streets and roamed the countryside. Nearly every family suffered losses from hunger and disease. Port cities overflowed with people who had the means to emigrate. The workhouses remained overcrowded. Even the jails were filling up.

If a revolution broke out, British leaders feared that the Irish ratepayers would not support the government. They knew that the landlords and large farmers were angry about Britain's relief policies, which forced them to pay rates they couldn't afford. To prevent any possible uprising, the British Parliament enacted the Treason Felony Act in April 1848. Under this law, any person who attempted to intimidate the British government was guilty of a felony, punishable by transportation for fourteen years or for life. The British government also sent ten thousand troops into Dublin, well supplied with arms and ammunition.

Undaunted, the Young Ireland leaders continued to hold meetings and make speeches against the British government. Determined to squelch the Young Ireland movement, the British authorities arrested its three leaders: William Smith O'Brien, Thomas Francis Meagher, and John Mitchel.

Speedy trials were held. When juries acquitted O'Brien and Meagher, British authorities were outraged at the upset. To make sure that Mitchel wasn't acquitted, they blatantly packed the jury with men who would find Mitchel guilty. It worked. Mitchel was found guilty of treason and sentenced to fourteen years' transportation to a penal colony in Australia and hard labor. On July 8, 1848, Charles Gavan Duffy was arrested, and another warrant was taken out for the arrest of William Smith O'Brien.

The Young Ireland leaders realized that time was running out. They had two choices: either drop plans for a rebellion or start the rebellion immediately, before plans were ready.

Young Ireland had no headquarters, no general, no military command, no strategy, and no stores of arms or ammunition. They also did not have the support of the Catholic Church. Under pressure from the British, Pope Pius IX forbade the Irish parish priests from becoming involved in political activity. The Pope told the priests that they would be guilty of provoking murder. Many parish priests agreed that the Irish laborers were unprepared for war.

Regardless of the lack of organization and support, Young Ireland decided to begin the revolution as soon as the potato harvest was over. The plans reached Duffy, who was in jail. He longed to escape, but all he could do was wait and hope that the uprising was successful—against the great odds.

A BOOTLESS STRUGGLE

Forty-five-year-old O'Brien had never desired the leadership role thrust upon him, but he accepted it. It is also likely that he never wanted a war. He probably hoped that an armed demonstration would bring the British government to reason. On July 23, 1848, he left his wife and five children in Cahirmoyle, County Limerick, and set off on horseback across the south of Ireland. He was determined to rally the Irish laborers and muster a large insurrectionary force.

As O'Brien traveled throughout the countryside, people cheered, waved green boughs, and lit bonfires in his honor. He delivered fiery speeches to the large crowds that greeted him. He told the laborers that Ireland's land system needed reform. It was the only way to save the people from death, hunger, destitution,

William Smith O'Brien and his fellow leaders traveled across the south of Ireland, stopping at Callan, Carrick, Cashel, Killenaule, Mullinahone, and Ballingarry to rally a rebel army. ILLUSTRATED LONDON NEWS, *AUGUST 12, 1848*

and eviction. He told the tenants that they were entitled to rights, that they should be compensated for improvements they made to their landlord's property, and that they deserved the security of leases and fixed rents to protect them from eviction.

Encouraged by the cheering crowds, O'Brien believed that the laborers and middle class wanted a revolution. He asked them to pledge their support to the cause. He told the married men to stay home with their families and working men to remain at their jobs, but he implored the single, unemployed men to join his army. It was to be a gentlemen's army: O'Brien forbade the ransacking of private property.

When the laborers pledged their support, O'Brien told them to go home, supply themselves with three days' worth of bread and biscuits, and come back prepared to fight. Many recruits never returned. As a member of the privileged landlord class, O'Brien did not understand that the laborers couldn't get bread and biscuits. They had joined his army in hope of getting food.

O'Brien also did not know that the parish priests worked against him. After he left each gathering, the priests urged the laborers not to rebel. The priests agreed that an army of emaciated laborers could not win. "It was not becoming for a priest to begin a bootless struggle," explained one priest. Without the priests' support, it was questionable whether a rebellion could ever succeed.

On Saturday, July 29, O'Brien heard that a police column was approaching Ballingarry. Two hundred men and women prepared to defend the little village. They barricaded the main street, then took their positions. About twenty men had guns, and they stood watch on the hillocks. About eighty men armed with pikes, scythes, and pitchforks held station in the ditches. The remaining men and women hid in the ditches, prepared to throw stones.

As the police column approached Ballingarry, Inspector Tom Trant, the commanding officer, spotted the barricade through his spyglass. He ordered his men to form the line. The police line advanced, and the rebels could barely contain their excitement. They shouted and jeered at the police and readied themselves, eager to fight. Without warning, the police broke rank. They wheeled a sharp right and ran, double-time, toward a two-story stone farmhouse set on a hill in the distance. The house belonged to Widow McCormack.

The main street of Ballingarry, shown here, was blocked by the rebels. ILLUSTRATED LONDON NEWS, *AUGUST 12, 1848*

The rebels couldn't believe their eyes: they had routed the police! The police were fleeing! Without waiting for orders from O'Brien, the rebels scrambled from the hillocks and ditches. They raced up the hill to cut off the police.

THE IRISH ARE NOT COWARDS
It is not known exactly how Widow McCormack found out that something was terribly wrong at her house. She may have spotted the rebels chasing the police, pitchforks and scythes in hand. She may have heard the gunfire. Or a passerby may have told her. However the widow found out, she rushed home to find her

After the police barricaded themselves in the McCormack farmhouse, the short-lived uprising took place. ILLUSTRATED LONDON NEWS, *AUGUST 12, 1848*

windows barricaded with furniture and bristling with guns. A battle was taking place in her front yard, and her children were nowhere in sight.

The frenzied mother ran to the garden gate and shouted to the police inside the house. She pleaded with them to cease fire and let her see her children. The police refused, but they told her to tell the rebels that they would negotiate.

The widow agreed to act as go-between. She looked for the rebel leaders and spotted a man creeping near the garden gate. It was William Smith O'Brien, inching his way closer to the house. She called to him, begging him to order a retreat. When he refused, she told him that her children were prisoners in the house. She asked him to find some way to protect her children and rescue them. Hearing this, O'Brien agreed to speak to the police.

O'Brien led Mrs. McCormack around the back of the house, where three men were trying unsuccessfully to set fire to a stack of hay. They hoped to smoke the police out. O'Brien ordered them to stop. "Here is the Widow McCormack," he said, "and she has been sent round by the police to say they will make terms."

It was dangerous to approach the house, but Widow McCormack followed O'Brien to a window that was barricaded at the bottom but open at the top. While Widow McCormack stood near, O'Brien climbed onto the windowsill and shouted to the police through the opening: "I want you to give up your arms, we will not hurt a man of you, you are Irishmen."

The police could have shot O'Brien, but they didn't. Instead, several police-men stretched their hands through the window, and O'Brien shook their hands, saying, "It is not your lives we want but your arms we want." It is not clear what happened next: either the rebels hurled rocks at the gable end of the house, strik-ing the house and shattering more windows, or the nervous police opened fire.

Whichever it was, a volley of shots from forty carbine guns rang out. Two men fell instantly, one dead and the other wounded. The rebels fired back, but they were outgunned. They dropped their pitchforks, scythes, and pikes. The rebel force scattered, falling on each other as they ran. Some ducked behind the stone wall. Others hid in ditches and in an old lime kiln a short distance away. "Wher-ever there was a hollow, people rolled into it to get cover," a reporter later noted.

The other rebel leaders urged O'Brien to call the men off. They advised him to fall back to Ballingarry where they could rally. He refused, saying, "An O'Brien never turned his back on an enemy." He mounted a captured police horse, probably Inspector Trant's, and rode to the ditches and lime kiln where his army had taken cover. He made a speech, but the rebels were not persuaded. O'Brien had no choice but to leave the field.

The Uprising of 1848 was over. In all, the police fired two hundred and fifty

Once William Smith O'Brien learned that the McCormack children were hostages, he agreed to make terms with the police. Here, O'Brien is shown reaching through the window to shake hands with the constabulary. ILLUSTRATED LONDON NEWS, *AUGUST 12, 1848*

After a week in hiding, William Smith O'Brien was arrested at the railway station at Thurles, County Tipperary. ILLUSTRATED LONDON NEWS, *AUGUST 12, 1848*

cartridges, leaving two villagers dead and others wounded. William Smith O'Brien remained at large for one week as police and detectives combed the Tipperary countryside. He was arrested at a railroad station as he attempted to return home to his family. Thomas Meagher and Terrence McManus were also captured. The three men were tried and convicted of high treason. They were sentenced to be hung, drawn, and quartered.

It was a brutal and barbaric sentence, but the men refused to ask for pardons. Not wishing to make martyrs out of the rebels, the British government commuted the sentence to transportation for life. William Smith O'Brien, Thomas Meagher, Terrence McManus, and Charles Gavan Duffy were exiled to penal colonies in Australia.

Many considered the failed uprising a pathetic farce—a mere gesture against death and hunger, evictions and emigration. But one newspaper reporter, who arrived at the scene within twenty-four hours, marveled at the courage of the rebels and their leaders and the courage of Widow McCormack and her children. "The wonder of the uprising is, not that the wretchedly armed peasants did not take the house from the police," said the reporter for the *Illustrated London Weekly*, "but that they had the daring hardihood to attempt it. . . . The Irish are not cowards, and they know it."

But the British leaders did not admire their courage. They were furious at the ungrateful rebels who had dared to rise against them, the very people who had granted the Irish money, work, clothing, and food during the past three years. When Queen Victoria heard about the rebellion, she wrote, "The Irish should receive a good lesson, or they will begin it again."

Chapter 10.
Come to Cork to See the Queen

Arise ye dead of Skibbereen
And come to Cork to see the Queen.

—DITTY SUNG IN THE STREETS, 1849

THE YEAR 1848 HAD a hopeful start, but it ended in double disaster. As police were combing the countryside for William Smith O'Brien and other leaders of the failed uprising, farmers and laborers were making a frightful discovery. The dreaded potato blight had returned, as virulent as 1846.

In August, heavy rain caused the blight to spread rapidly. Overnight, field after field of potato plants withered and blackened. Farmers dug the early potatoes and hurried them to market, but it was useless. Even potatoes that appeared healthy when dug soon melted into a stinking, rotten mass. By September, the potato crop was destroyed.

After the potato crop failed for the third time, another wave of emigration and eviction began. ILLUSTRATED LONDON NEWS, *FEBRUARY 9, 1850*

It rained still more throughout September, so heavily that farmers reported their cut hay was floating in the fields. Maggots and Hessian flies multiplied rapidly in the wet weather. The excessive rain caused wheat to sprout on the stalk and produced smut in the oats.

"The potatoes are gone as a crop," wrote Elizabeth Smith in her diary. "The corn much of it mildewed, and the hay partly uncut and partly lying in swathe under all these heavy showers. The cattle are not thriving. . . . Prospects for the winter are gloomy."

WORSE THAN GLOOM

The winter forecast was worse than gloom. The potato crop failure was a crushing blow to the Irish, but British leaders felt little sympathy. They were furious at the ungrateful people who had dared to rise against them. "We have subscribed, worked, visited, clothed, for the Irish," wrote Lord John Russell. "The only return is rebellion and calumny. Let us not grant, lend, clothe, any more and see what that will do." The consensus was that the Irish must take the consequences for their actions.

British leaders halted all extraordinary government relief measures, except for those measures already provided under the Irish Poor Law. They ended loans to the Irish unions and stopped shipments of clothing to the workhouses. If the Irish laborers needed workhouses and public works, let the Irish ratepayers shoulder the costs. To make sure they did, Trevelyan raised the rates.

The increased rates struck fear in the hearts of the rate-paying farmers. If they didn't pay, they knew that troops and police would seize their property, including whatever healthy grain was left. Without their grain crops, farmers couldn't pay their rent and faced certain eviction. In fear, many gave up their holdings and fled Ireland while they still had the means to emigrate. "They simply closed the door after them," explained William Blake. "They had little to bring and could not sell their farms."

Landlords faced the same dire circumstances. Without rents, they couldn't pay their rates, and they were in danger of losing their property. Some wished to sell their heavily encumbered estates, but the law required them to pay off all debts first. In despair, many abandoned their property and emigrated, leaving their lands to waste.

The new wave of emigration affected nearly every village and town, as large tracts of land were deserted. Without customers, shopkeepers and merchants closed their doors. City shops were shuttered up and broken windows stuffed with paper. Public houses closed. Notices and handbills were pasted over doors and walls. All over Ireland, the butter, bacon, and cattle trades foundered. Once-busy warehouses stood idle and empty on the quays.

The landlords and large farmers were negatively impacted, but small farmers and laborers suffered most of all. They couldn't afford to emigrate, since new legislation had increased the cost of passage. They could only suffer as the Poor Laws were strictly enforced. On the public works, older boys and men had to break stones for eight hours each day before they earned one pound of corn-meal. A priest described the workers as "stooping, feeble, ghastly scarecrows." The labor requirement was later raised to ten hours.

Masses of destitute people were turned away from the workhouses. For some people, jail became a place of refuge, where they were assured of one meal a day. To get arrested, they threw stones at street lamps or through shop windows in plain sight of policemen. Children and teenagers, desperate to leave Ireland, committed crimes and asked to be transported to penal colonies. One boy who got his request explained it this way: "Even if I had chains on my legs, I would have something to eat. Anything is better than starving and sleeping out at night."

The growing number of young convicts embarrassed British authorities, especially when the governors of penal colonies complained that the children behaved too well to be prisoners. The governors also said it wasn't fitting for children to mingle with older convicts and to be treated like common criminals. The British government realized that something had to be done.

LAND-GRABBERS

Just when it seemed as though life was hard enough for the farmers and landlords, it got harder. In an effort to even out Ireland's resources, the government passed the Rate-in-Aid, an act that required the more prosperous Irish unions to contribute financially to the distressed and bankrupt unions.

Ratepayers protested angrily: the rates had already been raised once, and now they were expected to pay more. They argued that it wasn't fair that Ireland was made to stand alone. They reminded the British government that the Act of Union had joined Britain, Scotland, and Ireland, and the three countries should contribute equally. But their protests fell on deaf ears. The Rate-in-Aid Act passed in May 1849, making Irish unions responsible for £322,000 in rates. It was the equivalent of about 1.5 million dollars.

The British government knew that increased rates weren't enough to save Ireland. They understood that many landlords did not have the money and could not afford to invest in their property. They also knew that many landlords wished to sell their estates.

The British government hoped to encourage wealthy British speculators to buy Irish land and invest money in improvements. They hoped that the new owners would improve the system of agriculture, so that crops other than potatoes would be planted.

To accomplish this, Parliament passed an amended Encumbered Estates Act in July 1849. (An earlier act had been passed in 1848.) Under this revised law, landlords were permitted to sell their estates without first paying off their debts. It also allowed the government to sell encumbered estates, even if landlords did not agree.

Because the value of Irish land had fallen drastically, people eagerly bought up land at bargain prices. To the government's dismay, new owners were not British, since few British people wanted to invest in a country as ruined as Ireland. Most buyers were wealthy Irish landlords or businessmen.

Other buyers were large farmers, called "land-grabbers." They bought their neighbor's land cheap when the neighbor died, emigrated, or was forced to sell his holdings for cash. "'Grabbing' was quite common," said Martin Breathnach, from County Kilkenny. "Farmers who had any money to spare were only too ready to approach the landlord or his agent and offer to pay back the rent if they would be given possession."

The new owners wanted empty land, so that they could expand their dairy

Brian Connor sits outside his scalp, near the Kilrush union workhouse in County Clare. During the Famine years, more than 250,000 people were evicted from their homes. ILLUSTRATED LONDON NEWS, *DECEMBER 22, 1849*

and livestock businesses. Ruthlessly, the new owners cleared the tenants from the estates, creating another wave of evictions. "No invader could be more heartless than some of the peoples' own neighbours," said Ned Buckley.

The British government had hoped that the Rate-in-Aid and the Encumbered Estates Acts would reform Ireland, but it didn't happen. Ireland was too far gone: twenty-two unions were bankrupt. Forty to fifty more unions verged on ruin. Two hundred thousand inmates were crammed into workhouses intended for 114,000. Inmates were fed just enough to avoid death by starvation. Inside and outside the workhouses, people were dying from starvation and disease.

"People were worn out with untold hardship," said Kathleen Hurley. "My father said he saw people dead on the roadside, such sights, their bodies all skin and bones, with bunches of green grass in their mouths, the green juice of the grass tricking down their chins and necks."

By 1849, Ireland proved too devastated for charities to continue relief operations. Since the blight first struck in 1845, private charities had donated more than one million pounds—nearly five million dollars—toward Irish relief, and now their funds and energy were gone. By June, the Society of Friends also withdrew their help from Ireland. Politely but firmly, they explained that the distress had grown beyond their ability to help. They also said that the British government was capable of raising the money and devising a plan to save Ireland. In all, the Quakers had spent over two hundred thousand pounds—about one million dollars—and countless hours over the Famine years.

Céad Míle Fáilte

Lord Clarendon, the Lord-Lieutenant of Ireland, offered an unusual remedy for the country. He suggested that a visit from Queen Victoria might serve as a tonic for the Irish people. He believed that a royal visit might boost Irish morale and stimulate Irish trade.

Clarendon's idea was remarkable, considering the bitterness harbored by the

Lord Clarendon hoped that a royal visit from Queen Victoria would boost the spirits of the Irish people and stimulate trade. ILLUSTRATED LONDON NEWS, *AUGUST 4, 1849*

Irish toward the English and the present state of Ireland. In Britain, Queen Victoria was popular and admired. She was young, now thirty years old, agreeable, and devoted to her husband, Prince Albert, and their six children. But how would the Irish people feel about the queen?

Lord Clarendon was convinced that she would be popular with the Irish. He believed that they would welcome a royal visit, since it would show that Queen Victoria hadn't forsaken them. He believed that the Irish would raise their hats to her and shout in Irish, "Céad Míle Fáilte" (pronounced KAYD MEAL-uh FALL-chuh), which means "a hundred thousand welcomes." Lord Clarendon began to make plans for a royal visit in August 1849.

Over the summer, Ireland prepared for the queen's ten-day visit. Though Lord Clarendon wished to keep expenses down, other officials undertook extravagant preparations. In Dublin, an army of Irish carpenters transformed the old city. They built balconies and tiers of elevated seats so that people could view the royal procession. They constructed triumphal arches through which the royal cortege would pass.

The lord mayor of Dublin planned for the entire city—the windows and the streets—to be illuminated for the queen. Merchants and peddlers sold gas devices, candles, and bucket lamps to light up windows and streets. Homeowners painted and decorated their houses, and shopkeepers washed their windows and set out their richest display of goods. People scrubbed and swept the streets, alleys, and courtyards. "There was never such scrubbing and beautifying, such running to and fro of busy men," said a reporter.

As the queen's arrival date grew closer, newspapers published lists of noblemen who arrived daily in Dublin. The city's milliners, tailors, and dressmakers were kept busy making hats, suits, and gowns for the ladies and gentlemen who hoped to be presented to the queen. Hotels and lodging houses filled up, and people rented out rooms and beds in their homes. They even sold window space to tourists who wanted to watch the royal procession. For security, extra troops were brought in and encamped in Phoenix Park, outside Dublin.

An Irish carriage-maker was commissioned to build an expensive, royal blue carriage to transport the royal family. He painted the royal arms on the panels and lined the interior with royal blue cloth. The royal blue wheels were intertwined with white. "It was an exquisite specimen of Irish manufacture," declared one newspaper.

Some people criticized the queen's pending visit. One newspaper editorial

The royal procession passes through a triumphal arch in Dublin. The queen's carriage cost more than £500, more than $2,500. ILLUSTRATED LONDON NEWS, *AUGUST 11, 1849*

pointed out that Queen Victoria would not see the worst areas in Ireland. She would not witness the wretched, starving peasants, the roofless cabins, the evicted tenants, the workhouses crammed with inmates. Others also criticized the extravagant amount of money spent on the preparations, especially as thousands of destitute Irish people lay dying from starvation and disease.

One man pointed out that nearly every poor family in Dublin had lost a parent

or child to disease. "If we have funds to spare, let them be spent not on illuminations but on her Majesty's starving subjects," he declared.

Other people, remembering the hundreds of people who had perished in
Skibbereen, sang: "Arise ye dead of Skibbereen/And come to Cork to see the
Queen." Some suggested that a funeral procession would offer the best greet-
ing from a famine-striken land.

HER MAJESTY WAS VERY MUCH PLEASED

Excitement won out. On Thursday evening, August 2, crowds lined the Cork
harbor. When the royal yacht appeared, warships and batteries shot off cannon
in the queen's honor. Bonfires burned on hilltops, rockets blazed in midair, and
the whole town was lit up.

On one estate, overenthusiastic servants used too much tar and kindling
wood for their bonfire and accidentally set fire to fourteen acres of fir trees.
Unaware of the accident, the queen thought the huge fire burned in her honor.
"Her Majesty was very much pleased with the effect," said a newspaper reporter.

The next morning, the river was filled with steamers, brigs, sloops, and
yachts, and thousands of people lined the harbor banks, eager to see the queen
and the royal family. As the queen appeared on deck, a band struck the national
anthem and everyone sang "God Save the Queen."

The queen boarded a small tender and toured the Cork harbor, then landed
in Cobh. Loud cheers and huzzahs resounded when she set foot on Irish soil. As
she stood on a specially built pavilion, she was presented with a pocket hand-
kerchief. It had been embroidered for her by students at the Cork Embroidery
School, one of the many industrial schools established for starving children.

The children also made a beautifully worked shirtfront for Prince Albert and
a frock for one of the princesses. "The frock was worked by a girl who could not
hem when she entered the school two and one-half years ago," noted a reporter.
"It is hoped that the fashionable of Cork will not now be ashamed to wear or

To impress the queen, people spent a great deal of money on fireworks and other illuminations. When the royal yacht appeared in the Cove harbor on August 2, the harbor was lit up. ILLUSTRATED LONDON NEWS, *AUGUST 11, 1849*

purchase articles similar to those admitted into the Royal wardrobe." Before she departed from Cobh, the queen renamed the town "Queenstown."

The royal yacht arrived in Kingstown harbor on Sunday, August 5. The next morning, small boats circled the royal yacht, with passengers waving laurel branches. The queen appeared on deck briefly, wearing a large red plaid shawl

In Kingstown Harbor, the crowds cheered as the queen presented the royal children:
Edward VII, age eight; Albert, age five; Alice, age six; and Victoria, age nine.
ILLUSTRATED LONDON NEWS, *AUGUST 18, 1849*

and plain straw bonnet. As the crowds cheered, she bowed several times in acknowledgment.

In Dublin, Queen Victoria attended a banquet at the Vice-Regal Lodge, which had been cleaned up for the occasion. She rode through the city streets in her carriage and passed under the triumphal arches. She watched a huge military exhibition in Phoenix Park and saw spinning and weaving displays at the Linen Hall in Belfast. Though she enjoyed the events, she was most amused when an Irish couple broke into a spontaneous jig, danced to the music of a piper.

Here, Irish couples delight the queen by performing a jig. ILLUSTRATED LONDON NEWS, *AUGUST 18, 1849*

It was just as Lord Clarendon had hoped: during the visit, Queen Victoria and the Irish people became enchanted with each other. She said she felt deeply for their suffering. In a letter to her uncle, she noted the thin and ragged people who cheered her each day. "You see more ragged and wretched people here than I ever saw anywhere else," she wrote. "The women are really very handsome—quite in the lowest class—such beautiful black eyes and hair and such fine colours and teeth."

The royal visit ended on August 12, when the royal family boarded their

Queen Victoria and Prince Albert wave goodbye to the Irish people as they board the royal yacht in Kingstown Harbor. ILLUSTRATED LONDON NEWS, *AUGUST 11, 1849*

yacht at Kingstown. The Irish people lined the harbor to wave goodbye, and the queen said that she left Ireland with "real regret."

For ten days, the royal visit brought pageantry and excitement to Ireland, but the visit had no long-term effects. As the 1849 harvest season approached, the famine was far from over. Victoria, queen of the mightiest empire in the world, could not provide a remedy for Ireland.

Conclusion

It stuck in my mind all these years . . .

—A TRADITIONAL WAY TO TELL AN OLD MEMORY

THE POTATO BLIGHT STRUCK again in 1849, but the crop failure was confined to areas in the west and south of Ireland. Elsewhere the harvest was mostly healthy. By 1850, the worst of the Famine was over.

Over the next fifty years, the blight struck several more times, but never as ferociously as during the Famine years. The potato eventually recovered its former strength, and for thirty more years, laborers and small farmers continued to rely on the potato as their staple food.

In 1850 the right to vote was extended to farmers who held twelve acres of land or more. This allowed middling farmers to join together with the large farmers to lobby for change. Small farmers, laborers, and women were still denied the right to vote.

In 1853 the British government canceled the four million pound debt that the Irish ratepayers owed. In all, the British spent about seven million pounds—

about thirty-five million dollars—on Famine relief. Another seven and one-half million pounds—over thirty-seven million dollars—came from emigrants who sent remittances home. Irish landlords and farmers contributed the greatest amount of relief to the Irish poor, about eight million pounds—nearly forty million dollars—through donations and the Poor Rate collections.

My Mother Did Not Know Me

The Great Irish Famine changed Ireland forever. It swept away whole families and villages. It nearly wiped out the Irish language and centuries-old traditions and folk beliefs. Some even say it killed the fairies. "There were fairies in Ireland then," said Diarmuid O'Donovan Rossa, near the end of his life. "Yes, English tyranny killed out the 'good people' as well as the living people." Others believe the fairies fled with the vast number of emigrants.

Most historians place the number of those who died at over one million and those who emigrated at about two million. Exact numbers will never be known, since so many people disappeared without a trace. We can follow Tom Quin, the young boy who waited eight days for his mother's coffin, as far as the Ennis union workhouse. No workhouse, parish, or later census records reveal whether Tom and his brother James survived.

The trail of Bridget O'Donnel, the young mother who refused to give up her cabin, goes a bit further. Though the whereabouts of her husband are not known for certain, it seems probable that he emigrated to the United States sometime before the eviction. An 1850 shiplist shows that a thirty-year-old Bridget O'Donnel and at least one daughter, age six, traveled from Ireland to Liverpool and then on to New York City several months after they entered the workhouse. It is possible that Bridget's husband found work and sent passage money for his family.

In 1863, at age thirty-two, Diarmuid O'Donovan Rossa took a trip to America and visited Philadelphia, where his mother and brothers and sisters had set-

A lone man walks through the devastated village of Tullig, County Clare. "No con-queror ever left more conspicuous marks of his devastation," said one reporter about the landlords who evicted the tenants. ILLUSTRATED LONDON NEWS, DECEMBER 15, 1849

tled. "It was night-time when I got to my brother's house," he said. "My mother did not know me. She rubbed her fingers along my forehead to find the scar from when I was a child. Nor did I well know my mother. When I saw her, with a Yankee shawl and bonnet, [she looked] as old as my grandmother."

Diarmuid returned home to Ireland, where he founded a nationalistic group that later became known as the Fenians. Its members believed that Ireland's future depended upon ridding themselves of the British. In 1869 he was jailed for his beliefs. While in jail, he was elected to Parliament, but he could not take his seat. Upon his release, he headed for the United States, and in 1871, he ran against the colorful politician "Boss" Tweed for New York state senator. Diarmuid's victory was thwarted by voter fraud. He then edited a weekend newspaper, the *United Irishman.*

In 1854, Young Ireland leader William Smith O'Brien was released in poor health from the Australian penal colony. He was granted a full pardon in 1856, and he returned home to Ireland as a hero. He died eight years later. Thomas Francis Meagher and Terrence McManus escaped from the penal colony to the United States in 1852. McManus settled in San Francisco, where he later died in poverty. Meagher rose to be a general in the Union Army during the Civil War. After the war, he was appointed temporary governor of Montana. He died in an accidental drowning in the Missouri River.

While in prison, John Mitchel wrote a book called *Jail Journal,* which would inspire future Irish nationalists. In 1853 he escaped to the United States and founded a newspaper in New York, in which he defended slavery and bitterly criticized his former Young Ireland comrades. He returned to Ireland twenty-seven years later, where he was elected to Parliament. He died soon after the election.

Charles Gavan Duffy argued his freedom from the Dublin prison in 1849. Three years later he was elected to Parliament, where he lobbied unsuccessfully for the Land Reform Bill. The bill was intended to give tenants compensation for improvements to their property and protection from eviction. Duffy later emigrated to Australia. He was appointed minister of the Province of Victoria and was knighted by Queen Victoria in 1873. The story is that Queen Victoria was astonished to discover that Sir Charles Gavan Duffy was the same man who had been convicted of treason.

During the month of August 1848, Katty McCormack and her family appeared in several newspaper articles. Later, the McCormack name appears only briefly in history books. Today, the McCormack farmhouse is known as the "War House" and is maintained by Ireland as a national monument.

THE LEGACY OF THE FAMINE

One effect of the Famine was the bitterness and resentment it left behind. Tom Flynn, the young man who emigrated to Canada after he poisoned his landlord's fish and later settled in the United States, never forgave the British government for its treatment of the Irish people. He passed his bitter feelings along to his children and grandchildren.

"As children we drew in a burning hatred of British rule with our mother's milk," said Tom's granddaughter, Elizabeth. "Until my father died, at over eighty, he never said 'England' without adding 'God damn her.'" Perhaps it is no surprise that Tom's granddaughter Elizabeth Gurley Flynn became a prominent American labor leader. For most of her life, she fought for better living and working conditions for men, women, and children.

Another lasting effect was the scattering of the Irish people. For the next sixty years, emigration continued at a high rate, accounting for half of each rising generation. The Famine emigrants helped cities develop and grow as they fulfilled the need for immigrant labor in the United States, Australia, Canada, and Britain. By 1910, five million people had left Ireland for good. Today, Ireland's population numbers about four million, less than half the amount in 1845.

In the United States, more than forty million people claim Irish ancestry. Though initially Irish immigrants faced prejudice, discrimination, and homesickness, their determination won out. Over time, they formed a large percentage of the American labor force, and they rose to the highest positions in labor, trades, politics, the military, the labor movement, the arts and entertainment industry, and other professions.

Most Irish emigrants never forgot their homeland, and they retained their ethnic identity and pride. "When we left Ireland, I was a baby," said one man from Richmond, Virginia, whose parents had emigrated during the Famine years. "My folks had hard times there, but my mother was always talking about the blue mountains and the lakes, and she never stopped loving it. She was always singing Irish songs around the house."

That the Irish people managed to hold onto their language, their songs, their poetry, their storytelling, and their desire for freedom is testament to their spirit and strength. A rebellion failed in 1916, but most of Ireland won its independence from Britain in 1921. Today, twenty-six counties are known as the Republic of Ireland. The tricolored banner that O'Brien carried home from France in 1848 became the flag of the Irish republic. The remaining six counties form Northern Ireland, still under the administration of the United Kingdom. In 1998, Northern Ireland was allowed its own Parliament in Belfast.

When bad things happen, it is human nature to search for something good to result. It is difficult to find anything good about a disaster as tragic and avoidable as the Great Irish Famine. But tragedy can teach us.

More than one hundred and fifty years have passed since the Famine. From this event, we can learn that the Famine is about individuals like Diarmuid O'Donovan Rossa, Tom Quin, and Bridget O'Donnel. We can empathize with their suffering. We can explore the complex means through which they and countless others attempted to survive and preserve their dignity. We can learn from their strength and courage.

Like Nicholas Cummins, the popular magistrate who carted bread to the people in Skibbereen, we can learn that famine is about society in crisis. It is about people who have access to food and people who do not. We can open our eyes to the hunger, poverty, and inadequate healthcare that exist today in our communities, our nation, and our world. We can respond more effectively to hunger, poverty, and human suffering.

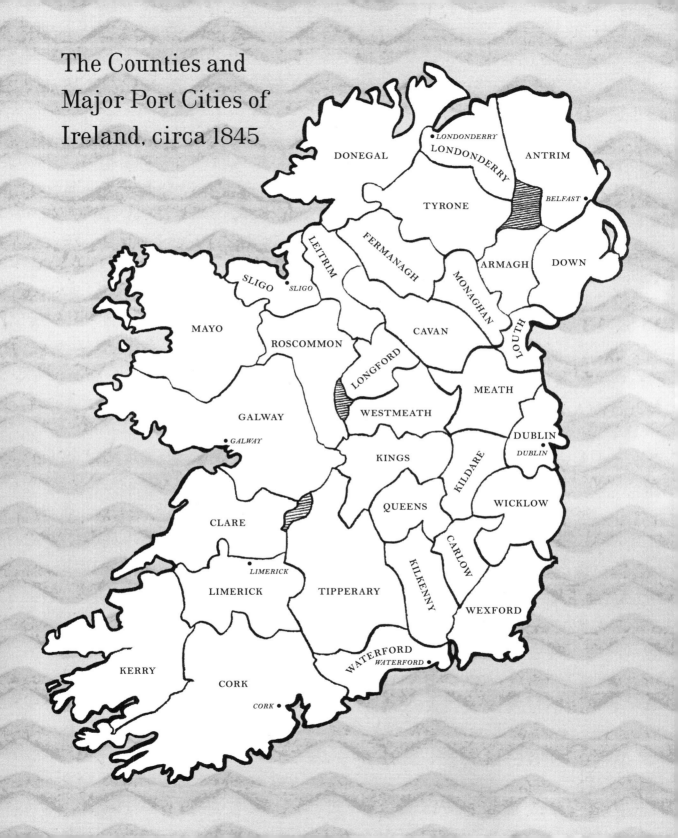

The Counties and
Major Port Cities of
Ireland, circa 1845

DONEGAL

LONDONDERRY
• LONDONDERRY

ANTRIM

TYRONE

BELFAST •

LEITRIM

FERMANAGH

ARMAGH

DOWN

SLIGO
• SLIGO

MONAGHAN

MAYO

ROSCOMMON

CAVAN

LOUTH

LONGFORD

MEATH

GALWAY
• GALWAY

WESTMEATH

DUBLIN
• DUBLIN

KINGS

KILDARE

WICKLOW

CLARE

QUEENS

CARLOW

• LIMERICK

KILKENNY

LIMERICK

TIPPERARY

WEXFORD

KERRY

CORK

WATERFORD
WATERFORD •

CORK •

Timeline

AUGUST 1845: First report of potato blight in Ireland.

OCTOBER 1845: One-third of the total crop lost.

NOVEMBER 1845: Peel orders purchase of £100,000's worth of Indian corn from the United States and establishes Relief Commission.

DECEMBER 1845: Food prices double, and 86,900 deaths are reported by Census. (Census figures here and elsewhere are likely to be underestimated, since it was not compulsory to record births or deaths before 1864.)

MARCH 1846: Public works schemes approved. Sale of Indian corn begins.

JUNE 1846: Peel wins lobby to eliminate duties from Corn Laws, then resigns as prime minister. Russell replaces Peel.

JULY 1846: Potato crop appears healthy. Parliament closes down relief committees. Trevelyan announces public works to end in mid-August.

AUGUST 1846: Blight reappears. Three-quarters of crop lost. Emigration escalates. Public works begin again.

NOVEMBER 1846: Abnormally severe winter sets in. Fever and dysentery are epidemic. The Society of Friends (Quakers) establishes a relief committee.

DECEMBER 1846: 390,000 people employed on public works. Census reports 122,899 deaths.

JANUARY 1847: British Relief Association forms.

FEBRUARY 1847: Soup Kitchen Act passed.

MARCH 1847: 714,000 people employed on relief works.

APRIL 1847: Fever Act passed to cope with epidemic.

JUNE 1847: Soup kitchens open.

JULY 1847: Soup distributed to three million people daily. A new Poor Law Act is passed, containing the "Gregory Clause" or "Quarter Acre Clause," resulting in wave of evictions.

AUGUST 1847: Little evidence of blight detected, but harvest is one-quarter the normal size and too small to sustain population.

OCTOBER 1847: Soup kitchens close. Large-scale emigration continues late into the year.

DECEMBER 1847: Crime and Outrage Bill passed. Emigration records estimate 220,000 left Ireland in 1847. Census reports 249,335 deaths.

APRIL 1848: Treason Felony Act passed.

JULY 1848: Two-thirds of potato crop destroyed. The funds and resources of the British Association run out. Young Ireland Uprising takes place in Ballingarry, County Tipperary.

SEPTEMBER 1848: Parliament halts extraordinary government relief measures. Poor Law rules strictly enforced and rates raised. First Encumbered Estates Act passed.

NOVEMBER 1848: Cholera epidemic begins.

DECEMBER 1848: Census reports 208,252 deaths. 180,000 emigrate in 1848.

MAY 1849: Rate-in-Aid Act distributes rates equally over all Poor Law unions.

JUNE 1849: Society of Friends gives up relief work.

AUGUST 1849: Queen Victoria visits Ireland. Potato blight confined to west and south.

DECEMBER 1849: Most workhouses full. Evicted families total 16,686 in 1849. An estimated 220,000 emigrated. Census reports 240,797 deaths.

1850: The right to vote is extended to thousands of farmers who hold twelve acres or more. Census reports 164,093 deaths. 210,000 emigrate.

1851: Census reports 96,798 deaths.

1852: Census reports 80,112 deaths. Outdoor relief phased out. An estimated 250,000 emigrate.

1853: The British government cancels the £4 million debt that Irish ratepayers owe.

1871: Census reports the population of Ireland as 4,412,000 — half that of pre-Famine years.

1916: On Easter Monday, a small rebel force of 1,500 fighters engages in a six-day battle for independence from Britain. The Irish rebels lose. Their fourteen leaders are imprisoned, secretly tried, and swiftly executed.

1918–21: Irish fight the War of Independence. The Anglo–Irish treaty of 1921 grants independence to twenty-six of Ireland's thirty-two counties, forming the Republic of Ireland. The remaining six counties form Northern Ireland, still under the administration of the United Kingdom.

1998: Northern Ireland voters ratify an agreement separating them from the Republic of Ireland and from Britain. Though still administered by the United Kingdom, Northern Ireland has its own Parliament in Belfast.

Bibliography and Sources

The Great Irish Famine lives on in countless stories, ballads, poems, and in the cultural memory of the Irish people. The sources listed below are intended to refer interested readers to more detailed historical works and to provide helpful information on the various works consulted in the research and writing of *Black Potatoes*.

Histories on the Famine tend to fall into three broad groups: nationalist histories that accuse the British government of genocide, revisionist histories that argue that the British did everything possible to save lives, and other revisionist histories that present findings relatively free from extremist views. The most well known work is Cecil Woodham-Smith's best-selling *The Great Hunger, Ireland 1845–1849* (London, 1962). The chapters dealing with the pre-Famine years are outdated, but Woodham-Smith's detailed account of the Famine is valuable for its graphic description of events. Other older standard works are R. Dudley Edwards and T. Desmond Williams's *The Great Famine: Studies in Irish History* (Dublin, 1956) and Rev. John O'Rourke's *The History of the Great Irish Famine of 1847* (Dublin: James Duffy and Co., 1902).

More recent perspectives and up-to-date research on the Famine can be found in Mary Daly's *The Famine in Ireland* (Dublin Historical Society, 1886), Joel Mokyr's *Why Ireland Starved: A Quantitative and Analytical History of the Irish Economy, 1800–1850* (London: George Allen and Unwin, 1983), and Christine Kinealy's recent *A Death-Dealing Famine* (Chicago: Pluto Press, 1997) and *This Great Calamity* (Boulder, Colo.: Roberts Rinehart Publishers, 1995). Also valuable are essays found in *Fearful Realities: New Perspectives on the Famine* (edited by Chris Morash and Richard Hayes, Dublin: Irish Academic Press, 1996) and *The Making of Modern Irish History: Revisionism and the Revisionist Controversy* (edited by D. George Boyce and Alan O'Day, London: Routledge 1996).

The Irish famine has been well documented, thanks to its timing (relatively late in western history) and its geography (within the United Kingdom), and we have many accounts from the British. We can look to charity records, newspaper reports, reports of the Poor Law inspectors, minute books of the various Union Boards of Guardians, workhouse records, official government documents, and in diaries, letters, and memoirs in which the lives of the ordinary Irish are briefly mentioned by members of the middle and upper classes. Other valuable primary sources include census records, parish records, charity records, land and property records, and tax records such as Griffiths Primary Valuation. Such records offer the researcher ample raw material for both analytical and narrative purposes.

Noel Kissane's *The Irish Famine: A Documentary History* (Dublin: National Library of Ireland, 1995) provides an excellent and diverse collection of reprinted primary documents and images from travelers, government authorities, civil servants, botanists, reporters, and bystanders. Additional documents can be found through an Internet search. (Ireland's County Clare Library offers a wealth of information at its Web site, which I located at www.clarelibrary.ie.) Many of these records can also be obtained from the Family History Library, Salt Lake City. Operated under the auspices of the Latter Day Saints Church, the Family History Library offers an extensive microfilm and microfiche collection of genealogical records. Lending branches of the Family History Library are found in many local Latter Day Saints churches.

I also consulted books such as *The Letters of Queen Victoria: A Selection from Her Majesty's Correspondence Between the Years 1837 and 1861* (edited by Arthur Christopher Benson, et al., New York: Longmans, Green and Co., 1907), *Sir Robert Peel, from His Private Correspondence* (edited by Charles Stuart Parker, London: John Murray, 1891), Sir Charles Trevelyan's *The Irish Crisis* (London: Macmillan and Co., 1880), and Elizabeth Smith's *Irish Journals, 1840–1850* (New York: Oxford University Press, 1980).

Several writers traveled throughout Ireland to provide firsthand accounts of life in Ireland. In addition to travel articles published in various contemporary newspapers and magazines, Arthur Young's *A Tour in Ireland* (1780) and S. C. Hall's *Ireland* (London: Hall, Virture, and Co., circa 1860) offer pre-Famine views of Ireland. Alexander Somerville's *Letters from Ireland During the Famine of 1847* (Portland, Ore.: Irish Academic Press, 1994), Aesnath Nicholson's *Lights and Shades of Ireland* (London: Charles Gilpin, 1850), and Lord Dufferin and the Honorable G. F. Boyle's *Narrative of a Journey from Oxford to Skibbereen* describe the graphic Famine conditions found in Ireland.

I also relied on contemporary newspapers and periodicals. I found Bridget O'Donnel's story in the *Illustrated London News* (December 22, 1849) and Tom Quin's story in the *Clare Journal* (November 27, 1848; December 11, 1848; January 11, 1849). In addition to these newspapers, I used the London *Times*, the *Pictorial Times*, the *Clare Journal*, the *Cork Examiner*, the Dublin *Evening Mail*, the *Edinburgh Review*, the New York *Mercantile Advertiser*, and the *American Whig Review*. Since photography was in its infancy, newspapers such as the *Illustrated London News* and the *Pictorial Times* were especially valuable for their contemporaneous illustrations.

Social behaviorists claim that it takes seven generations to breed out overt behavior patterns caused by deep emotional trauma. One hundred and fifty years after it struck, the Famine lives on in the cultural memory of the Irish people. It is embedded in the way they live, love, hope, and believe. With this in mind, I chose to tell the story of the Famine through the eyes and memories of the Irish people, wherever possible and wherever verifiable. Because many Famine victims were non-English speaking and illiterate, written documentation is scarce. Though many refused to speak of their suffering, others passed on their memories to their children and grandchildren. Tom Flynn's story was told by his granddaughter Elizabeth Gurley Flynn in her autobiography, *The Rebel Girl: An Autobiography of My First Life* (New York: International Publishers, 1955). Diarmuid O'Donovan Rossa wrote *Rossa's Recollections, 1838–1898* (Shannon, Ireland: Irish University Press, T. M. MacGlinchy Publisher, 1972) late in his life.

During the 1930s, 1940s, and 1950s, fieldworkers for the Irish Folklore Commission went out into the Irish countryside and collected the memories from the children and grandchildren of the Famine victims. Thanks to the Irish Folklore Commission, Ireland has a rich folk memory collection. Though it's impossible to recapture the lives of the ordinary Irish exactly, the folk memories provide us with thousands of manuscript pages and thousands of hours of sound recordings on gramophone discs and tapes. These folk memories describe traditional customs and beliefs, folktales, and historical events such as the Famine. The memories are preserved and available to scholars and to the general public in the main manuscript collection of the Department of Irish Folklore, University College Dublin, Ireland. Though many are written in Irish, many are also written in English. Some have been published in Cathal Póirtéir's work, *Famine Echoes* (Dublin: Gill Macmillan, 1995). In addition to the Irish Folklore Commission manuscripts, I also used oral histories collected during the 1930s in the United States by fieldworkers for the Works Progress Administration. The easiest way to locate the WPA histories is by visiting the American Life History collection at the Library of Congress Web site at www.lcweb.loc.gov. (Specific documentation for the above can be found at the end of the bibliography.)

Information on cultural memory and the Famine can be found in Margaret Kelleher's *The Feminization of Famine: Expressions of the Inexpressible?* (Durham, N.C.: Duke University Press, 1997), various essays in Tom Hayden's *Irish Hunger: Personal Reflections on the Legacy of the Famine* (Boulder, Colo.: Roberts Rinehart Publishers, 1997), and Christopher Morash's *Writing the Irish Famine* (New York: Oxford University Press, 1995).

Emigration is discussed in most of the secondary sources mentioned earlier. I relied on those texts as well as Kerby Miller's *Emigrants and Exiles: Ireland and the Irish Exodus to North America* (New York: Oxford University Press, 1985), Arnold Schrier's *Ireland and the American Emigration, 1850–1900* (Minneapolis: University of Minnesota Press, 1958), and Hasia R. Diner's *Erin's Daughters in America* (Baltimore: Johns Hopkins University Press, 1983). One source that may be difficult to find but worth the effort is Edith Abbott's *Historical*

Aspects of the Immigration Problem (Chicago: University of Chicago Press, 1926). This work contains reprints of many primary articles on the subject of immigration. Irish emigrant passenger lists can be found in *The Famine Emigrants: Lists of Irish Immigrants Arriving at the Port of New York, 1846–1851* (Baltimore: Genealogical Publishing Co., 1985).

Firsthand accounts of coffin ships can be found in Robert Whyte's *Famine Ship Diary* (edited by James J. Mangan, Dublin: Mercier Press, 1994). The author was a cabin-class passenger who kept a diary of his travel from famine-stricken Ireland to Canada in 1847. The diary first appeared in print in 1848 under the title *The Ocean Plague: The Diary of a Cabin Passenger*. Another important document that describes the deplorable steerage conditions is a letter written by Stephen De Vere. A wealthy member of an Anglo-Irish family who was concerned about emigration conditions, De Vere took steerage passage from Ireland to Canada. He described the trip in detail to T. F. Elliott, the chairman of the Colonization Committee. The easiest way to find this letter is to conduct an Internet search, using Stephen De Vere's full name. (I found it at www.swan.ac.uk.history.) Another good Web site on Grosse Isle is found at www.ist.uwaterloo.ca/ ~marj/genealogy/ships1866.html.

Information about Irish folklife and folkways, hedge schools, souperism, evictions, workhouses, public works, diseases, and burials can be found in many of the primary and secondary sources already mentioned. Additional essays include Kevin Whelan's "An Underground Gentry? Catholic Middlemen in Eighteenth Ireland," J. R. R. Adams's "Swine-Tax and Eat-Him-All-Magee: The Hedge Schools and Popular Education in Ireland," and Gearóid Ó Crualaoich's "The Merry Wake," all found in J. S. Donnelly Jr. and Kerby A. Miller's *Irish Popular Culture, 1650–1850* (Portland, Ore.: Irish Academic Press, 1999). Irene Whelan's "The Stigma of Souperism" and James S. Donnelly Jr.'s "Mass Evictions and the Great Famine" are found in *The Great Irish Famine* (Dublin: Mercier Press, 1995), edited by Cathal Póirtéir. For more information on Irish folklife, read Mary Murray Delaney's *Of Irish Ways* (1973; reprint, New York: Harper and Row, 1980), Kevin Danaher's *In Ireland Long Ago* (Dublin: Mercier Press, 1964), and Olive Sharkey's *Old Days, Old Ways* (Syracuse: Syracuse University Press, 1987).

Other sources consulted on Irish folklife were manuscripts from the Works Progress Administration Federal Writers' Project. The manuscripts are located in containers 740 and 752 in the Manuscript Division, Library of Congress, Washington, D.C. Two classic sources on the fairy faith are Professor W. Y. Evans-Wentz's *The Fairy Faith in Celtic Countries* (University Books, 1966) and Lady Gregory's *Visions and Beliefs in the West of Ireland* (1920; reprint, New York: Oxford University Press, 1970). The daughter of a resident Anglo-Irish landlord, Augusta Gregory grew up loving the fairy stories told to her by her Irish nurse. As an adult, she learned the Irish language and collected the folk stories from the farmers, potato diggers, beggars, and elderly people in the workhouses.

Eyewitness accounts of Young Ireland and the Uprising of 1848 can be found in Sir Charles Gavan Duffy's *Four Years of Irish History, 1845–1849* (New York: Cassell, Petter, Galpin and Co., 1883), Thomas Francis Meagher's *Meagher's of the Sword: Speeches of Thomas Francis Meagher, 1846–1848* (edited by Arthur Griffith, Dublin: M. H. Gill and Son, 1916), John Mitchel's *Jail Journal, or Five Years in British Prisons* (New York: Woodstock Books, 1996), and in Reverend P. Fitzgerald's *Personal Recollections of the Insurrection at Ballingarry* (Dublin, 1868). Katty McCormack's account was published in the *Illustrated London News* (July 29, August 4, 12, 1848). Well-documented secondary sources on the subject include Richard Davis's *The Young Ireland Movement* (Dublin: Gill and Macmillan, 1987), Denis Gywnn's *Young Ireland and 1848* (Cork, Ireland: Cork University Press, 1949), Robert Sloan's *William Smith O'Brien and the Young Ireland Rebellion of 1848* (Dublin: Four Courts Press, 2000), and Blanche M. Touhill's *William Smith O'Brien and His Irish Revolutionary Companions in Penal Exile* (Columbia: University of Missouri Press, 1981).

For readers interested in helping people who suffer from hunger, poverty, and inadequate healthcare, a good place to start is your local telephone book. Under the listings for "human services," you'll find organizations such as the American Red Cross and the United Way. You'll also find the names of faith-based organizations such as the Catholic Charities, Lutheran Welfare, and the Salvation Army. These groups provide services such as food pantries, food kitchens, and shelters. You can also find information on the Internet at the Web site for the United Nations (www.wfp.org/index.htm).

I wish to thank Professor Séamus Ó Catháin, head of the Department of Irish Folklore, University College Dublin, for his permission to quote from the main manuscript collection.

In the original manuscript collection, some names appear in English and others in Irish. For ease in reading, I have taken the liberty of translating the Irish names into English. The original Irish names and their translations (where applicable) are listed below. All translations are of my own rendering.

Volume 415: Kathleen Hurley (p. 92)

Volume 1068: Connor O'Neill (Conchubhair Ó Néill, p. 289), Thomas Kelly (Tomás Ó Ceallaigh, p. 289), Mary Murphy (Máire Bean Uí Mhurchadh, pp. 272–73), Shane McCarthy (Seaghan Mac Cártha, p. 251), Margaret Donovan (Maighreead Ní Dhonnabháin, p. 154), Martin Breathnach (Mairtín Breathnach, pp. 103–4)

Volume 1069: Felix Kernan (pp. 34, 36, 37), Louis O'Malley (Lughaidh Ó Maollumhlaigh, p. 166), Thomas O'Flynn (pp. 356, 371), Sean Cunningham (Seán Mac Cuinneagáin, p. 62), Mrs. Lennox (p. 18), Francis Mac Polin (p. 23), Kathleen Donovan (p. 137), William

O'Flynn (p. 355), Johnny Callaghan (p. 255), John Phillips (p. 293), William Powell (pp. 235–36)

Volume 1071: Sean O'Dunleavy (Seán Ó Duinnshléibhe, pp. 10–11), Ned Buckley (pp. 112, 113, 126, 133, 149), Séamus Reardon (pp. 253, 256, 259), John McCarthy (p. 274), Sean Crowley (pp. 295, 303)

Volume 1072: Hugh O'Hagan (p. 406), Thomas Kelly (p. 114), Jimmy Quinn (pp. 393–94), Mary Nugent (p. 330), Jane O'Kane (pp. 260, 270)

Volume 1073: Patrick Dempsey (Pádraig Ó Diomasaigh, p. 376)

Volume 1074: Michael Gildea (p. 448)

Volume 1075: P. Foley (pp. 143–44), Mrs. G. Kirby (pp. 10–11), William Keane (p. 493), Mrs. Fitzsimons (pp. 527–28), William Blake (p. 153), Mick Kelley (p. 471), Barney Gargan (p. 602), John Hanrahan (p. 119), Brigid Keane (p. 442), Brigid Brennan (pp. 14–15), Mrs. Kavenagh (p. 180), Mrs. Gilmore (p. 559), James Doyle (p. 172), Charles Clarke (p. 630)

Volume 1344: Richard Delaney (p. 456)

Volume 1358: Joseph Doherty (Seosamh Ó Dochartaigh, p. 178)

Index

Act of Union, 15–16, 141, 156
Aherne, Johnny, 9
"American Wake," 120–21
Argue, James, 78
Australia, 73, 83, 132–33, 134, 143, 170

Ballingarry rebellion, 136–48
Black fever (typhus), 95
Blake, William, 154
Bog squatters, 23–24
Breathnach, Martin, 156
Brennan, Brigid, 51
British Relief Association, 65, 83
Buckley, Ned, 23, 81, 99, 110, 158

Callaghan, Johnny, 90–91
Canada, emigration to, 1, 85, 115–16, 117, 119, 121
    sailing conditions, 128, 130, 132
Catholic Church, 1, 28, 29, 141, 143
    Irish members leave, 70, 78–80
    laws against, 13, 15–16
    -Protestant conflict, 13, 78–80
Catholic Emancipation Act (1829), 16
Celebrations, 24–25
Children, 68–70, 72, 77, 81–82
    emigrant orphans, 132
    starving, 97, 155, 162
Choctaw Nation, 83
Church of England, 13
Clarendon, Lord, 158–60, 165
Clarke, Charles, 115
"Coffin ships," 128, 130, 132

Connor, Brian, 157
Connors, Sean, 113
Cork Embroidery School, 162
Corn, importation of, 40–41, 43–46, 51, 55, 59
    "Peel's brimstone," 46, 50
Corn Laws, 40–41, 43–44, 49
Crime, 70–74, 155
Crime and Outrage Bill, 116
Crowley, Sean, 94
Cummins, Nicholas, 63–64, 65, 67, 172
Cunningham, Sean, 75

Delaney, Richard, 99
Dempsey, Patrick, 71
Deruane, Old, 53
Disease, 1, 92, 94–103
    "ship fever," 116, 128, 130
Donovan, Kathleen, 87
Donovan, Margaret, 103
Dougherty, Joseph, 117
Doyle, James, 103
Duffy, Charles Gavan, 141, 143, 151, 170

Edgeworth, Maria, 20
Emigration, 1, 117–35, 142, 153, 154–55, 172
    American relatives aiding, 118, 130
    emigrants contribute to famine relief, 85, 168
    landlord-assisted, 115–16, 118
    mortality rate, 132
    numbers of emigrants, 117–18, 130, 132, 168, 171
Encumbered Estates Act, 156, 158
England

contributes to famine relief, 83, 85, 151, 167–68, (stops) 154
government attitude, 35–36, 53, 55–56, 59–60, 65, 67, 107, 154, (acts and bills passed) 74–77, 100, 116, 125, 142, 155–56, 158 (see also Penal Laws; Poor Law Acts) and Irish emigration, 118
    Irish emigration to, 132
    Irish rebellion against, 136–51, 154, (fears of) 116, 135
    laissez-faire economics of, 41, 51, 56, 67
English-Irish conflict, 11–16, 141–51, 171
Evictions, 104–16, 144, 153, 157–58, 169

Fairies, belief in, 9, 10, 29, 53, 168
Farm laborers. See Laborers
Fenians, 170
Ferguson, Samuel, 104
Flynn, Elizabeth Gurley, 72, 135, 171
Flynn, Tom, 72, 130, 132, 133, 135, 171
Foley, Mr. (farmer), 8
Food prices, 61–62
France, 135, 141–42

Gargan, Barney, 17–18
Gearins, Tom, 103
Gilmore, Mrs., 72
"Gombeen men" (moneylenders), 33

Grain harvest and exports, 55–56, 58–59, 64, 71
"Gray Man," 9
Great Famine, 1, 3
    British attitudes toward, *see* England
    famine relief, 73–88, 168
    grain and livestock exports during, 55–56, 58–59, 71
    Ireland changed by, 168
    legacy of, 171–72
    lessons from, 172
    mortality rate during, 69, 92, 94, 168
    population before, 17
    riots during, 57–59
    worst is over, 167
    See also Potato blight
Gregory, William, and Gregory Clause, 107, 113

Hanrahan, John, 47
Hedge schools, 27
Hefferman, Pete, 29
Henry VIII, king of England, 13
Home rule, 141, 172
Housing, 22–24
Hughes, James, 24
"Hungry months," 29, 32, 51
Hurley, Kathleen, 158

Illustrated London News, 65–67
Illustrated London Weekly, 151
Indian corn. *See* Corn
Industrial Revolution, 19
Ireland
    British rule of, 19, 28
        Irish hatred of, 13, 16, 171
    -England conflict, 11–16, 141–51
    history of, 25, 27, 28
    and independence (home rule), 141, 172
    Irish elite rule of, 15
    maps of, 12, 173
    population of, 1, 17–19, 171
    poverty in, 1, 18–20, 28, 29–31, 142
    rebellion in, 136–51, 154, 172
        feared, 135
    Republic of, 172
    in United Kingdom, 15–16, 172
Irish Board of Works, 46–47, 60
Irish Fever Act, 100
Irish language, 1, 27, 172
    forbidden, 27
Irish Parliament, 141

Jail Journal (Mitchel), 170

Kavenagh, Mrs., 72
Keane, Brigid, 47
Keane, William, 31
Kelly, Mick, 47
Kelly, Thomas, 80
Kennedy, Capt. Arthur, 115
Kennedy, "Little Miss," 81, 82
Kernan, Felix, 61, 75
Killian, Jim, 113

Laborers, 20–25
    marriage and family life, 27–29
    potato crop failure and, 32–36
    public works for, *see* Public works
Labour Rate Act, 59–61
Laissez-faire economics, 41, 51, 56, 67
Lalor, James Fintan, 141
Lamartine, Alphonse de, 141–42
Landlords, 11, 19–20, 21, 27, 31
    emigrants' fear of, 119
    emigration of, 154
    evictions by, *see* Evictions
    export food during Famine, 55–56
    and famine relief, 80, 81, 168
    and Irish rebellion, 145
    and land-grabbers, 155–58
    and public works, 46, 60
    Protestant, 15, 16
Land Reform Bill, 170
Lincoln, Abraham, 135
Livestock exports, 55–56, 59

MacAirt, Cormac, 136
McCarthy, John, 94
McCormack, Widow and children, 136–40, 145–48, 149, 151
    house of ("War House"), 171
McDonald, Daniel, 10
McKennedy, Denis, 49
McManus, Terrence, 141, 151, 170
MacPolin, Francis, 80
Mahon, Major Dennis, 115–16
Mahony, James, 45, 65, 66, 67, 96
Malnutrition, 92, 97
Malone, Thomas, 49
Mansfield, John, 35
Marriage and family life, 28–29
Meagher, Gen. Thomas Francis, 141, 142, 151, 170
Mitchel, John, 141, 142–43, 170
Mortality rate, 69, 92, 94, 132, 168
Murphy, Mary, 78

National School system, 27
Northern Ireland, 172
Nugent, Mary, 95

O'Brien, William Smith, 141, 142–51, 152, 172, 176
O'Connor, Rev. B., 70
O'Donnel, Bridget, 104–7, 110, 113, 168, 172

O'Donovan Rossa, Diarmuid, 7,
    8–9, 11, 27, 53, 121,
    168–70, 172
O'Dunleavy, Sean, 21, 110
O'Flynn, Thomas, 72, 95, 102
O'Hagan, Hugh, 61
O'Kane, Jane, 119, 123
O'Malley, Louis, 68
O'Neill, Connor, 121
Orphan emigration scheme,
    132–33
Osborne, Rev. Sidney Godolphin,
    97

Passenger Acts (U.S. and
    Britain), 125–28, 133
Peel, Sir Robert, 36, 37, 38,
    40–41, 43–44, 49, 51
    "Peel's brimstone," 46, 50
Penal Laws, 13, 15
Phillips, John, 127
Pitt, William, 15
Pius IX, pope, 143
Poorhouse. See Workhouse
    system
Poor Law Acts, 30, 31, 81, 89,
    115, 154, 155
Poor Rate collections, 168
Potato blight (1845 and 1846), 1,
    8–11, 53–54, 59, 140, 158
    earlier crisis (1816), 36
    and farm laborers, 32–36
    fungus causing, 36, 38, 53
    as "God's will," 9–10, 11, 35,
    53
    returns, 152–54, 167
Potatoes as food, 2, 6–8, 20, 51,
    167

Indian corn as substitute for,
    40, 43–46, 51, 55, 59
    planting season, 24
    rotten, 8–10, 39, 40
Powell, William, 10, 55
Protestantism, 13, 141
    conversion to, 78–80
Public works, 46–49, 135, 154,
    155
    closed, 53
    reinstated, 60, 61
    replaced by soup kitchens, 77

Quakers. See Society of Friends
Quarter Acre or Gregory Clause
    (1847), 107, 113
Quin, Tom and family, 100, 102,
    168, 172
Quinn, Jimmy, 94

Rate-in-Aid Act, 155–56, 158
Reardon, Séamus, 110
Rice, Bess, 113
Russell, Lord John, 51, 52–53, 59,
    135, 154

Scalps (shelters), 22, 23, 27, 98,
    112, 113
Sheedy, Dan, 106
Skibbereen, 63–64, 67, 101, 103,
    172
    workhouse, 92
Smith, Elizabeth, 81, 153
Society of Friends, 82–83, 84, 158
Soup kitchens and "souperism,"
    73, 75–77, 78–80, 84,
    86–88
Soyer, Alex, 76

Temporary Relief Act ("Soup
    Kitchen Act,"), 73, 75–77
Trant, Inspector Tom, 139, 145,
    148
Treason Felony Act, 142
Trevelyan, Sir Charles, 52–53,
    59, 73, 88, 154
Turf-cutting, 24–25
Tweed, "Boss" William Marcy,
    170

United Irishman, 170
United Kingdom, 15–16, 172
United States
    and famine relief, 83, 85, 133
    Irish emigrants in, 1, 85, 117,
    119, 133, 135, 171–72
    passes Passenger Act (1847),
    133

Victoria, queen of England, 15, 42,
    43, 65, 83, 135, 151, 170
    visits Ireland, 158–66
Voting rights, 13, 16, 167

"War House," 171
Weather, 5, 8, 61–62, 67
Wellington, Arthur, Duke of, 65
Whyte, Robert, 125
William III (of Orange), king of
    England, 13
Workhouse system, 30–31, 75,
    88, 107, 133, 154
    overcrowded, 89–92, 112, 115,
    142, 155, 158
    workhouse coffin, 100, 102

Young Ireland, 140–43, 170